Furniture Flips

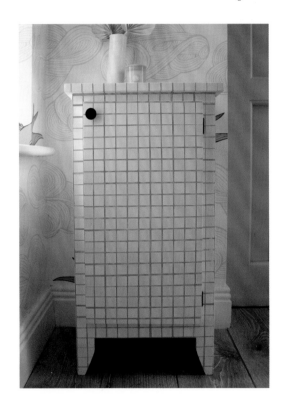

Furniture Flips

25 bright and vibrant painted furniture projects

Joanne Condon

CICO BOOKS

LONDON NEW YORK

Published in 2023 by CICO Books
An imprint of Ryland Peters & Small Ltd
20–21 Jockey's Fields, London WC1R 4BW
341 E 116th St, New York, NY 10029

www.rylandpeters.com

10 9 8 7 6 5 4 3 2 1

A CIP catalog record for this book is available from the
Library of Congress and the British Library.

ISBN: 978 1 80065 215 6

Printed in China

Editor: Sophie Devlin
Designer: Alison Fenton
Photography and illustration: Joanne Condon
Senior commissioning editor: Annabel Morgan
Art director: Sally Powell
Creative director: Leslie Harrington
Production manager: Gordana Simakovic

Contents

Introduction

Furniture flipping, also known as upcycling, is the art of turning an old piece of furniture into something new. You can change its function to suit your needs, or simply add a coat of paint to enhance what's already there, give it a new look and increase its value. To me, it is the best fun you could ever have. And when your family and friends come to visit and ask where you got that amazing piece of furniture, there is nothing more satisfying than being able to say: 'I flipped that.'

Secondhand furniture is filled with character and may have lived for many lifetimes before it comes to you. Pieces that might otherwise be sent to landfill and replaced can instead be mended, painted, stripped back and painted again. It is a much more sustainable way to personalize your home and generally costs a fraction of the price.

Furniture flipping is a form of art, and every piece is a blank canvas on which to express yourself. However, you do not have to be an experienced artist or maker to get into upcycling. The 25 projects in this book are arranged in order of complexity and each one comes with step-by-step instructions and photographs that will guide you along the way. Once you are familiar with the basic techniques, you can start to really enjoy the process and let your personality shine through. Painting furniture in the colours that make you happy will really lift your mood.

When you are flipping a piece, your main goals should be to have fun and to create something you love, so try not to get too fixated on making absolutely everything perfect. Experimenting is part of the fun – it's why, after 14 years of painting furniture, I'm still excited to get up in the morning and start something new. During a project, you will be so close to the piece, looking at every brushstroke and every tiny flaw, and that can help you get into the habit of creating the best finish you possibly can. However, these objects aren't brand new and shiny: we can work on them to make them the best they can be, but perfection is not the end goal. Even if things don't work out exactly as you planned, at least you will have learned something new.

My other piece of advice is to make sure you give yourself plenty of time to complete a project. Putting yourself under pressure to paint something in a single day or in a weekend won't lead to the best results, and it isn't going to give you the chance to enjoy the process either. This book will help you get the techniques right, but the most important thing is that you see this as a fun activity and the end result will be that you get to use, enjoy and show off that piece of furniture in your home.

I hope that this book brings you lots of inspiration and helps you to look at old furniture differently, whether you're a complete beginner or an experienced upcycler. As you develop your skills and grow in confidence, feel free to take elements from different projects and mix them together with your own ideas to create something completely new. The only limit is your imagination.

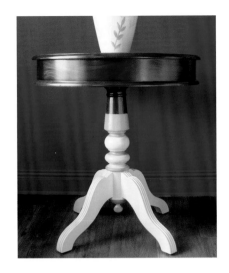

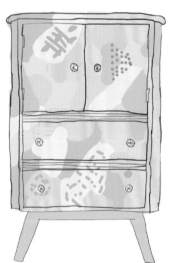

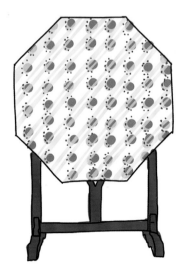

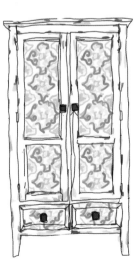

Sustainability

Flipping old furniture that is in need of some TLC will greatly minimize the waste that we create in our homes. Nowadays, most of us are familiar with the 'fast fashion' industry and what it is doing to our planet, but 'fast furniture' is also a huge problem and is one of the most rapidly growing landfill categories.

According to a report from the European Environmental Bureau, 10 million tonnes (around 11 million US tons) of furniture are discarded every year in Europe, and most of this is destined for landfill or incineration. The situation is just as bad in the United States, where the Environmental Protection Agency estimates that 12 million US tons (around 10.8 million tonnes) of furniture and furnishings are thrown away annually.

Trends in interior design are changing more rapidly than ever and fuelling demand for affordable, mass-produced furniture. As a result, many manufacturers have moved away from good-quality materials and fine craftsmanship. Cheap furniture is often hastily assembled and more likely to fall apart after only a few years, at which point it usually ends up in landfill – and if it is made of plastic, it will take hundreds of years to break down. Meanwhile, the owner goes out and buys something new, continuing the cycle. Because of how 'fast furniture' is made and its many design flaws, it can be very difficult to mend if you want to give one of these pieces a second chance at life.

By contrast, flipping old furniture has so many environmental benefits. For one thing, it slows down the demand for new furniture, which leads to a reduction in using raw materials and saves the world so much pollution.

Secondhand or vintage furniture, even if it is only a few decades old, is often made with great craftsmanship, holds loads of character and can be easily mended so that it lasts for many more years to come. For instance, I have painted kitchen chairs that were in use around a farmhouse table for 30 years and were still in near-perfect condition. A coat of paint gave them a modern feel at a fraction of the cost of buying new chairs. Decorating furniture the way you want to, changing colours with the years and not being chained to trends will not only help the environment but also keep more money in your pocket.

Painting can change the look of a piece completely and open our minds to being creative with the function of old furniture. Old wardrobes/armoires can become amazing pantries, dressing tables/vanities can become office desks and old drawers can even become dog beds. The possibilities are endless.

You can change the look of a piece of furniture by simply replacing the new legs or hardware. Keep the original components for future projects, as this can make for interesting results when different styles are combined together. Painting old handles is another possibility that can change them completely with minimal waste. Always remember that old furniture was made to stand the test of time. Reusing it is the best choice for our planet.

Sourcing Old Furniture

Hunting for treasure is my favourite part of the furniture-flipping process – it is so rewarding when you spot a hidden gem that's just waiting to be transformed into something new. There are many different places where you can find your next project, depending on where you live.

Charity Shops and Thrift Stores

My local charity shops are always the first place I go. Some specialize in furniture and homeware, but even those that mainly sell clothing might have a few pieces of furniture at the back of the shop. Donations come in all the time and the stock can change on a daily basis, so the key is to visit regularly – I go at least once a week.

Secondhand and Antique Shops

There are some really good deals in secondhand and antique furniture shops, but the best bargains may not be visible on the shop floor. I like to chat with the staff to see if they have anything in the back that may be a little damaged and in need of repair – if so, they may be willing to give you a discount.

Auctions

Auctions are where you can find truly one-of-a-kind pieces, sometimes at great prices. There is also the added bonus of being able to bid at auctions online now too. If possible, I like to physically go into the auction house to take a closer look at the pieces I'm especially interested in a few days before the bidding starts.

Flea Markets, Car Boots and Yard Sales

These are great places to pick up gems and have a rummage around to see what you can find. Some days you can find a hundred things you want and others you may find nothing at all, but it's a really fun experience to look at all kinds of pieces, both old and new.

Online

Big websites such as Gumtree, Preloved, Facebook Marketplace, Ebay, Etsy and Craigslist have so many bargains and even free items, although the choice can sometimes be overwhelming and you do have to consider how you will get your purchases home, especially if they are far away from where you live. There are also loads of different local buying and selling groups online that will help you pick up affordable pieces without having to go too far, and you can set up notifications to be alerted whenever something new pops up in the group.

Things To Look Out For

Before you buy a piece of secondhand furniture to flip at home, you need to look at it carefully – there are several different factors that you need to consider.

Woodworm

This is the first thing I look for in a piece of furniture I'm thinking about buying. If it's something for my own house, I have no problem with treating woodworm, although I tend to avoid it if I am flipping a piece to sell. Spotting woodworm can be difficult, but a handy tip is to use the light on your phone to help you peer into the darker areas.

I will check the whole piece, starting on the outside and then removing the drawers and checking each section. The first telltale sign of active woodworm is a really fine dust. Then you need to check for the exit holes. A lot of the time people treat only these holes for woodworm, but in fact the whole piece will need to be treated.

If the surface is heavily varnished or painted, you will need to sand it back before you apply the woodworm killer so the chemicals can penetrate the wood. Imagine the wood as a sponge that needs to soak them up. Before using woodworm killer, make sure you read the manufacturer's instructions and follow the safety guidelines.

Condition

Broken objects can be great candidates for upcycling, but you should factor the cost and time needed for repairs into the overall price. Consider whether you can fix the piece yourself or if you will need to pay someone to mend it for you. Another thing to look out for is water damage – look at the feet, underneath, round the back and inside for signs of mould. Musty smells inside cupboards or drawers can be easily got rid of by tipping some baking powder inside and leaving everything closed for 24 hours, then vacuuming up the powder. You may need to repeat this a few times in order to remove the odour completely.

Materials

Look to see what materials have been used to make the piece of furniture. Is it made from a hardwood such as oak or a softwood such as pine? Other materials you may encounter include MDF, chipboard and plywood. Any of these may be laminated or veneered to give them a different appearance. I would also see if the surface has been painted before. This adds extra work and time to strip it back, depending on how well it was painted by the previous owner. However, if this was a piece I really wanted, stripping it back would be worth it for me.

Build Quality

I will always look at how things are assembled, as this can give a clue to their age and quality. Using screws to hold everything together is a quicker and more modern way of assembling furniture, whereas traditional construction methods such as dovetail joints give the piece more longevity and can be easily mended to last years. They are also very appealing to look at.

Price

Although buying secondhand furniture can be a great way to save money, price is the last thing I look at. There are no rules or guidelines that determine how much is reasonable to pay for a particular piece – it really depends on how much you want it, and on the other factors I have discussed here. If it's a piece you have been searching for, and it fits exactly in a certain space or it has the label of a prestigious manufacturer, I would always be open to spending a little bit more for something special.

Common Repair Jobs

Using Wood Fillers

There are two types of wood filler that I use regularly when working with furniture. One is a pre-mixed wood filler that is perfect for refilling old handle holes and minor scrapes and dents. The other is a more robust two-part filler that has a paste and a hardener that needs to be mixed in a small amount before applying. This filler can be moulded and sanded once it is dry, and some brands can be tinted with a wood stain so that the filler blends in with the wood, which is useful if you want to leave the piece unpainted. Make sure you are wearing gloves and a mask in a well-ventilated area when using this kind of filler.

Sometimes you will find that wooden furniture has become chipped over time. It's most common in pieces that have a veneer finish – a thin layer of wood that is usually glued to a more inexpensive material. If the veneer is chipped and loose, it may need to be removed and then you can mend the area with wood filler.

With a scraper, fill the area with the wood filler – dipping the end of the tool in water can help the knife glide easily across the area you are filling. Try to remove as much excess of the wood filler as you can, as this saves you time when sanding it. Leave the filler to dry fully.

Sand off the wood filller until it is flush with the surrounding wood, then use 180 grit sandpaper to make the surface smooth and clean off the dust with a tack cloth. Then you can prepare the surface as normal (see page 14).

Clamps and Wood Glue

Some pieces of furniture might need a little bit of reinforcement to make them last longer. Glue in joints can dry out over time and may need to be reapplied. You will need to remove the old glue with a chisel first in order to achieve a good repair job.

Once the old glue is removed, dust the area and apply a good-quality wood glue. You need to clamp everything in place while the glue is drying. When you squeeze the clamp closed, it may push out the excess glue, so you will need to wipe this with a cloth before leaving it to dry. There are many different clamps available in a range of sizes.

Missing Moulding

Small sections of moulding might be missing from furniture, but you can make your own replacements using wood filler.

Clean the section you need to replicate and cover it in a wax to make sure your mould is easy to remove. Using a hot glue gun or mould putty kit, cover the whole of the area in glue or putty. This will cast that area and you can then use it to make the section that is missing.

Allow to completely harden. Then remove the glue or putty cast, making sure to do so it slowly and carefully. You will need to apply a wax inside the mould to ensure your new section will pop out easily. Next, use a two-part wood filler to fill the mould and create your new section of moulding, following safety precautions as before.

Once dry, pop it out of the mould and you can then sand the piece to make it fit. Glue with a strong superglue and hold it in place with painter's tape while it's drying.

Once the glue is dry, sand it with an 80 grit sandpaper to get it into shape and then use 120 grit to smooth it out. And then you are ready to paint.

Paints

There are so many paint brands on the market and so many different finishes that it can be really confusing. However, there are four main finishes that you need to know about – most brands will carry these, though they may call them by different names.

Matt
Matt paint has a flat finish with no sheen. It needs to be sealed with a protective wax or varnish and may not be durable enough to withstand everyday life. For this reason, I seldom use it on furniture.

Eggshell
Also known as mid sheen, this finish has a subtle reflective quality – slightly more than a matt paint, but less than satin. Like matt paint, it doesn't show too many flaws.

Satinwood
Sheen paint is often called satin or satinwood because it reflects light in a way that resembles the fabric of the same name. It can be easily cleaned and wiped without damaging the paintwork.

Gloss
Gloss is a highly reflective and shiny paint finish, especially if the paint is oil-based rather than water-based. It is easy to keep clean, but may show the smallest imperfections.

I need the paints I use to be good quality, easy to work with and durable and also affordable – though you cannot always measure this by looking at the price per can. If a paint is cheap but low in quality, you will need to apply more coats of the paint to get the same effect, meaning that it could cost more overall. By contrast, just 1 litre (around 1 US quart) of good-quality paint should be enough to paint a large wardrobe/armoire or six kitchen chairs. In my experience, cheap paints also tend to drip more easily, show every brushstroke and can discolour over time. For a list of my favourite brands, see page 156.

Some paint brands offer a 500ml can (around 1 US pint), which is great if you are using a few different colours on a project. However, the paint sold in tiny sample-size pots is usually intended for walls, so it won't be suitable for furniture projects unless it clearly states on the label that the paint can be used on wood. Most gloss and satinwood paints can be used for wood and metal and for interior and exterior items such as garden furniture. This means you can complete lots of different projects around your home with just 1 litre (around 1 US quart) of paint.

Another thing to consider is what your paints are made of. Most are either oil- or water-based – I like to use water-based formulas because they contain lower levels of harmful chemicals called volatile organic compounds (VOCs). Water-based paint also dries more quickly and is much easier to clean from your brushes after you have finished painting.

Preparing Furniture for Painting

No matter what type of paint you are using, preparing and priming the furniture correctly before you start painting will give you a more attractive and durable finish. It is the most important step, so don't be tempted to skip it – knowing that you have the right base will give you peace of mind as you embark on your project.

clean furniture with a sugar soap spray

wipe off the spray with a lightly dampened cloth

Cleaning

Always make sure you clean your piece of furniture thoroughly, even if it doesn't seem dirty. I normally use a spray bottle of sugar soap for this. Spray the soap onto your furniture and let it sit for a minute to break down the grime before you wipe it off with a lightly dampened cloth. Never use a wet cloth for this – you don't want to add moisture into the wood.

If your piece is extra dirty or has a waxy finish, you can use a product called Krud Kutter, which will remove the stubborn grime more easily and also strip away the waxy layer that can act as a barrier when you are priming. If you have sensitive skin, always make sure you wear gloves when using cleaning products.

Sanding

Sanding is the best way to prepare the wood so that your primer or undercoat will cling onto the slightly rough surface. A scuff sand is all you need to make sure the primer adheres correctly, so you don't have to completely remove the finish. However, if you miss an area of sanding or skip it completely, you risk the primer peeling and scratching off easily. You will not be able to fix this later, no matter how many layers of paint you put on afterwards, so take the time to sand the entire surface before priming.

When you are sanding, always work in the direction of the grain to avoid leaving deep scratch marks on the surface. Always wear a good-quality protective face mask when sanding, even outdoors.

I use a medium sanding block for all the awkward areas first. A sanding block is easy to control and makes it easier to get into hard-to-reach areas such as spindles on chairs. It also allows you to carefully sand more ornate areas such as mouldings and carvings, which might be damaged if you were to use an electric sander.

Then I move onto flatter areas with an electric sander. You can also do this by hand, but investing in an electric sander will save you a lot of time and elbow grease. Even if you are using a circular orbital sander, a sanding sponge disc can be very helpful when you need to sand curved areas, as it allows you to sand everything without damaging the edges.

dusting with a tack cloth removes any lingering dust

Next, you will need to clear the dust away. I do this using a vacuum cleaner fitted with the brush attachment. I do a lot of sanding at home, so I have a separate vacuum just for this purpose, but you can use your regular one. It's a great way of getting rid of the majority of the dust quickly.

After vacuuming, go in with a tack cloth and remove any lingering dust. This is a special cloth that is coated in beeswax to make it slightly sticky. You will be surprised by how much dust you pick up.

Sanding Grits for Painting Furniture

Coarse
80 Grit
This is for removing a finish, such as varnish or paint. It can also remove shallow scratches on the surface.

Medium
120 Grit
This is for prepping the surface before priming. It's the perfect grit for your primer to cling onto and will also remove any small imperfections in the wood.

Fine
180 Grit
This is for in-between coats of paint. It will remove any imperfections in the paint and help you achieve a perfectly smooth finish.

Ultra Fine
220 Grit
This is for wood that has been stripped back and needs a final sand to make it smooth. For an even smoother finish on wood you can go to a higher grit.

For electric sanders, you can pick up these grits in the form of mesh discs, which will save on sanding time compared with sandpaper discs. The mesh is also more economical and will last longer.

sanding block is
easier to control

using an electric
sander on flatter
areas saves time

a sanding sponge
prevents damage to
the edges of the wood

vacuuming with the brush
attachment quickly
clears the dust away

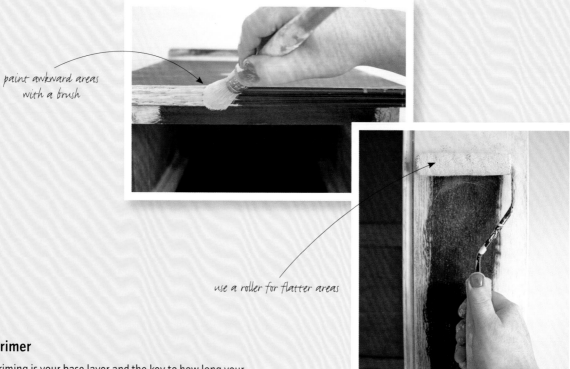

paint awkward areas with a brush

use a roller for flatter areas

Primer

Priming is your base layer and the key to how long your paint will last on your piece of furniture. The primer clings and adheres itself to the scuffs you have made at the sanding stage. The sanding and priming stages are the perfect combination for your base layer and will hold everything in place. If the piece has any hinges or areas that you don't want to paint, you should cover them with painter's tape before priming.

First paint all the awkward areas with a brush, then paint the flatter areas using a microfibre roller. Make sure you keep your roller light on the surface, as pressing too hard will leave raised lines on either side. If this happens, you can go over those lines with the roller again.

Once you have applied a good primer, you can paint almost any material. If the wood is bare, a layer of primer will prevent the paint from soaking into the wood. It can also be used as a stain block and will help paint adhere to shiny surfaces. You can get special primers that cover the knots in wood and prevent any bleeding. Some primers can even be tinted to help with coverage.

Undercoat

This can be used after a primer to improve the coverage of the paint, but on most projects it is not really necessary – the primer on its own will suffice. I would use an undercoat underneath white or light-coloured paint, where the coverage might be an issue, so that I don't have to apply so many coats of paint on top.

An undercoat can also be helpful if you want to improve the coverage of high-pigment colours such as yellow and red, or darker colours where there is a risk of the primer showing through. In this case, I would use a tinted undercoat in a similar colour.

Scratch Test

I have been painting for 14 years and will still always do a scratch test. This will flag any potential problems you may face before you start painting. Once your primer is dry, try to scrape it off. If the primer comes off, it isn't fully dry yet.

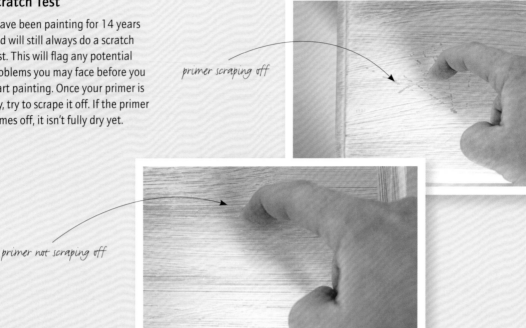

primer scraping off

primer not scraping off

Preparing Drawers

Drawers can present some challenges when they aren't prepared properly – sometimes they can become stiff and get stuck easily.

To avoid these problems, you can take a few extra steps when working with drawers. Unless the drawers are on a metal pull mechanism and have lots of room on either side, I avoid painting the sides. This is because I use water-based paints, which can cause the drawers to swell a little and make it hard to get them back into place, especially if they are already a tight fit. I do use painter's tape to keep the paint line straight so that there is a nice neat edge when you open the drawer. You can also use wood stain to refresh the drawer sides if they look a little worn.

The inside of the chest of drawers/dresser can also be taped off so that it has a nice crisp edge and the drawers can easily be pulled in and out.

add some painter's tape either side so that the drawers don't get stuck after painting

Removing Varnish

If you plan on not painting the wood or want to keep a section of it exposed, you will first need to remove the existing finish. The best way to remove a varnish is to give it a scuff sand and then strip it back using an eco-friendly paint stripper. Sanding will allow the paint stripper to penetrate the surface more successfully.

Always make sure when you are using a paint stripper that you are following the instructions and safety precautions on the packaging. Apply a thick layer of the paint stripper and let it sit for the recommended time.

Use a scraping knife to remove the varnish and carefully dispose of the waste by wrapping it in newspaper. Then use a stainless-steel scourer to remove any remnants.

Sand back the surface with a fine sanding paper and remove the dust with a tack cloth. Then you can apply a fresh coat of wood stain, oil or varnish as desired.

Removing Old Paint

Furniture dating from before the late 20th century may have lead in the paint, so it's important to be cautious and make sure it's safe to work on. You can buy testing kits and test an area before you begin working on it. If there is lead in the paint, you may have to abandon your project, as lead-based paint can be extremely dangerous.

If the paint is safe to work on, scuff sand the surface before applying a thick layer of eco-friendly paint stripper. Follow the manufacturer's guide for the amount of time you need to let it sit, then scrape it back with a scraping knife. Use a stainless-steel scourer to tackle any awkward areas.

apply a thick layer of paint stripper

use a scraping knife to remove the varnish

Painting

I always like to let the primer layer (and undercoat, if using) dry fully overnight before I start working on it again. It would be rare for me to apply a primer and two coats of paint in just one day. Each layer needs time to cure properly. Before you begin painting, look at your piece and sand back any drips or imperfections in the primer.

When you are painting, make sure you aren't applying too much paint to your piece. When you dip your brush into the pot or container you are using, wipe off the excess paint on the side. If there is paint dripping off your brush, you have picked up too much.

For better control of your brush when painting, keep your hand down close to the stainless-steel part of the brush so that the handle is resting on your hand.

Don't worry about your first coat of paint on your piece – I call this 'the ugly phase'. You will be questioning all your decisions at this point, but it's on the second coat that you will achieve full coverage and your piece will really start to look good. Two thin coats are better than one thick coat, but make sure you let each one dry properly in between.

Paint all the awkward areas first using a sash paintbrush. If it is a chair or small table, I would usually turn it upside down, paint all the fiddly areas that you can see first and then flip it over and repeat. For the larger areas I use a microfibre roller.

Leave each layer of paint to dry completely. For a super-smooth finish, sand with a 180 grit sandpaper in between coats. Repeat these steps for a second coat.

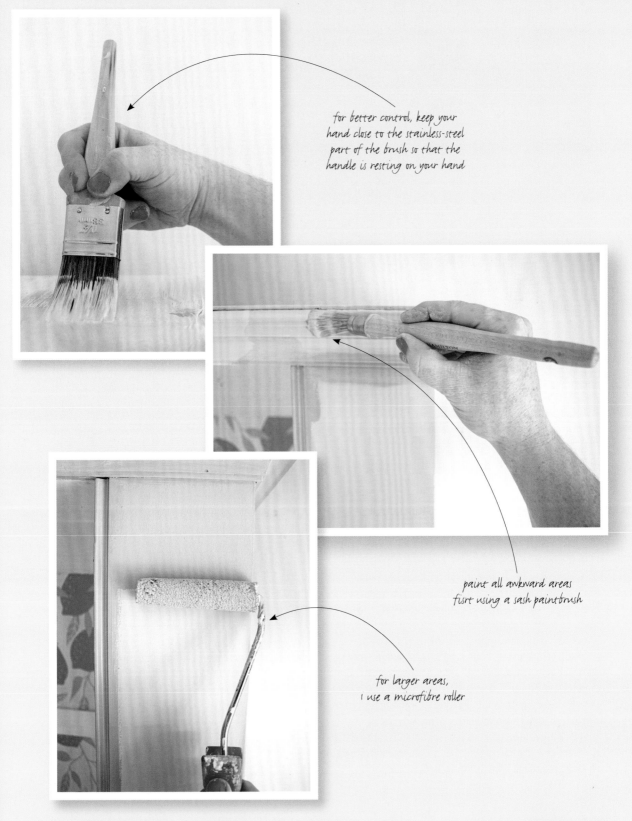

for better control, keep your
hand close to the stainless-steel
part of the brush so that the
handle is resting on your hand

paint all awkward areas
fisrt using a sash paintbrush

for larger areas,
I use a microfibre roller

choose a colour that you love, that makes your heart sing!

Choosing a Colour Palette

Colour can be a hard thing to nail down. There are so many options and potential combinations that many people find choosing colours incredibly difficult. Seeing all those colours on a paint chart, which is only really a fraction of what's available, can be confusing. Sometimes you think you've found the perfect colour, but once you see it in real life you aren't sure it's the same colour that you chose.

As a result, it can be tempting to play it safe. People often revert back to the old reliables – whites, greys, beiges and creams – to take away the stress of choosing. However, colour can add so much positivity to your life and it can be introduced in so many ways. Refreshing your furniture is a great alternative to painting the walls. If you're afraid, start by painting something as small as a stool, side table or plant stand. I bet that little stool you have painted will soon become your favourite thing to look at and bring a smile to your face. My other piece of advice is to look in your wardrobe/closet for colour inspiration. Perhaps there is a piece of colourful clothing that makes you happy and will lead you to the right hue for your furniture.

When choosing decorative materials for upcycling your furniture, whether it is fabric or paper, always choose that first and then a paint colour after. There are thousands and thousands of paints and it is easy to match it up to a textile or wallpaper. The other way around can be quite difficult, as there are more limitations.

Choose a colour that you love, that makes your heart sing. Not everyone will like this colour, but that's OK, unless you live with them of course! And even then, I have chosen paint colours that my husband didn't like at first, but once he saw the end result, he came around.

Keeping paint swatches of colours you like in a little box can be really useful. If you collect them over time, you will start to see tones and colours that you are drawn to. Taking these out and playing with colour combinations Is one of my favourite things to do.

Tool Care

Taking care of the tools you work with will make them last longer and keep them nice to use for many more projects in the future.

To make your brushes last for years and stay as good as new, I like to go in with a realy good eco-friendly brush cleaner and conditioner or a paintbrush soap. This cleans the brush but also brings the softness back into the brush so that the bristles don't dry out.

Lather your brush with the paint cleaner and conditioner and leave for about 2–3 minutes to break down the paint. Then rinse it under a tap and brush through again with a brush comb. Leave to dry by placing the brush bristle-side down. This prevents the water from breaking down the glue in the brush head and rotting the handle if it is made of wood. Once the brush is fully dry, you can then turn it bristle-side up for storage.

If you leave your paintbrush with paint on it overnight and it has hardened, you can still save it. A good paint cleaner and conditioner can have it looking like new again or by filling a jar with fabric softener and leaving the bristles to soak for 24 hours. This will break down the paint so that you can rinse It out and use the brush again. The earlier you do this, the better chance you have of completely saving your brush.

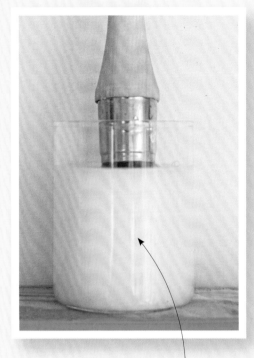

leave your brush to soak in fabric softener for 24 hours

always leave your brushes to dry bristle-side down and then store them the other way up in a pot

chapter 1

Easy Flips

Lucky Dip

A kitchen chair is one of the most versatile pieces we can have in our homes – not just in the kitchen or dining room, but in other spaces as well. This simple project, in which a chair is painted to look as though it has been dipped in colour, is perfect for beginners. You can use any hue you like, or paint several chairs in different shades for a mismatched look.

TECHNIQUE: dipping

MATERIALS

sanding block
painter's tape
primer
sash paintbrush
tack cloth
satinwood paint
clear, water-based varnish
painter's tape

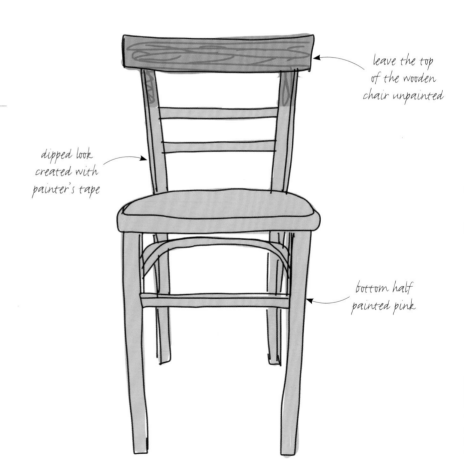

leave the top of the wooden chair unpainted

dipped look created with painter's tape

bottom half painted pink

1 The top of the chair will not be painted, so sand this area right back to remove all the varnish. Scuff sand the remainder of the chair so that the paint will adhere to the surface.

2 Using painter's tape, mark the line where you are going to paint from. Press down the edges of the tape firmly to prevent the paint from seeping underneath – this will ensure you get a clean line.

3 Now it is time to prime the lower part of the chair, up to the painter's tape. A sash paintbrush will give you the greatest control. There are lots of awkward areas to cover, so turn the chair upside down at first. Paint everything you can see, then flip it over to paint the rest. Leave to dry.

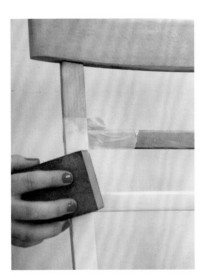

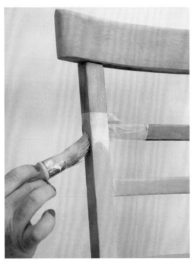

4 Sand back lightly to smooth any imperfections, especially any excess primer around the spools, then wipe away the dust using a tack cloth. This will help you achieve a better finish.

5 Paint over the primer using your chosen colour. As before, go over the painter's tape, without getting any paint on the area that will be left bare.

6 While the paint is still wet, slowly remove the tape to reveal the sharp paint line and the dipped paint look. Leave to dry completely.

7 This is optional, but if your chair has visible screws like this one, you can paint them the same colour as the chair base. Most satinwood paints are suitable for both wood and metal surfaces. Protect the surrounding wood with painter's tape, then prime and paint the screws. Leave to dry.

8 Seal the top of the chair with a clear, water-based varnish to protect the bare wood. Leave to dry completely and then your chair will be ready to use.

Handles With Flair

Updating the handles on a piece of furniture can make a huge difference. Old hardware can be given a new lease of life using spray paint or polish. However, sometimes you may fall in love with handles that don't fit the existing bolt holes. This filler trick is a handy solution that will allow you to change one bolt hole to two or vice versa – the choice is yours. This piece was originally a dressing table/vanity with a mirror, which I removed to turn it into a desk.

TECHNIQUE: changing handles

MATERIALS

screwdriver
wood filler and scraper
electric sander and sanding block
primer
paintbrushes
ruler
pencil
new furniture handles
drill and drill bit
vacuum cleaner
eggshell paint
metal polish
wallpaper and paste (optional)

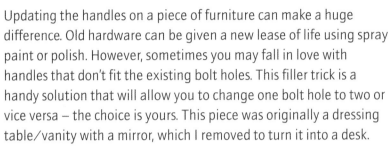

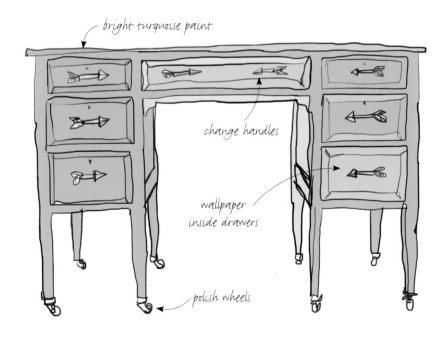

bright turquoise paint

change handles

wallpaper
inside drawers

polish wheels

1 Take out the drawers and clean them thoroughly, then remove the old hardware. It doesn't matter what holes the old handles have left behind, as these can be easily filled.

2 Using your finger, cover the existing holes with some wood filler. Use slightly more than you need to make sure the holes are completely filled.

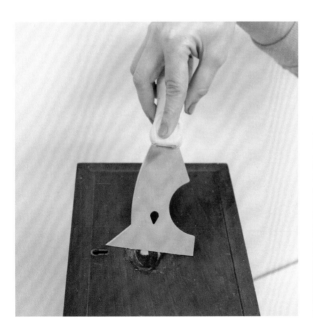

3 Use the scraper to remove the excess filler. Leave overnight until completely dry, then sand back the wood filler until it is flush with the surface of the drawer.

4 Prepare and prime everything (see page 14) and leave to dry. Carefully measure the drawers and position the handles where you want them, then use a pencil to mark where you plan to drill the new holes.

5 Using a drill bit the same thickness as the bars on your new handles, drill the new holes in the front of each drawer. Use a vacuum cleaner to clear away any dust or debris.

6 Now it is time to paint your furniture, allowing it to dry fully after each coat, and polish the wheels. You may also want to line the drawers with wallpaper (see page 62). Add the new handles and secure them in place.

Starburst Stencil

Inspiration for furniture flips can be found in many places. For instance, I am a lover of pottery – the different textures, the flecks in the clay and the glazed finishes. Here, I achieved a similar look by lightly washing the upper section of this table with a thin 'glaze' of satinwood paint so that the wood shows through. Meanwhile, the lower section looks as though it has been dipped in the glaze. The stencil resembles a pattern you might see on a ceramic mug. I also changed the drawer handle – for instructions, see page 32.

TECHNIQUE: stencilling

MATERIALS

painter's tape
electric sander and sanding block
primer
paintbrushes
satinwood paints, including white and black
dampened cloth
dry paintbrush or toothbrush
starburst stencil
stencil brush or round sponge
cardboard
artist's brush
clear, water-based varnish

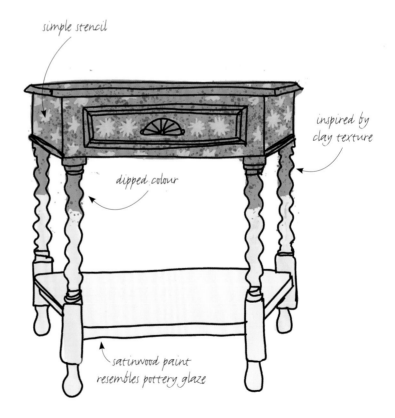

simple stencil

inspired by clay texture

dipped colour

satinwood paint resembles pottery glaze

1 After marking out the upper and lower sections of the table using painter's tape, strip and sand back the upper section until it is completely bare (see page 14). Prepare and prime the lower section and leave to dry, then apply two coats of white satinwood.

2 With a lightly dampened (but not wet) cloth, apply a thin coat of the same paint to the upper section and buff it out to achieve a whitewashed look. I worked on a small area at a time so that I would have enough time to buff the paint before it dried.

3 Once the white paint is dry, use a dry brush to flick black satinwood paint onto the whitewashed area to give it the textured look of clay. You could also use a toothbrush to achieve the same effect. Leave the paint to dry completely.

4 Securely tape your stencil in place with painter's tape. This will keep it from moving while you work and prevent any bleeding of the paint.

5 There are lots of different stencilling tools, but I prefer a stencil brush or a round sponge for control. Always remember to load up your tool and then offload. First, load up your brush or sponge with paint.

6 On a scrap piece of cardboard, offload the excess paint. This is the key to a good, clear print. You may think that there isn't enough paint left on the tool after you offload, but you really need to trust the process.

7 Apply a thin layer of paint through the stencil by tapping up and down – make sure you work your way around every part of the starburst design.

8 Carefully remove the stencil and leave the paint to dry – this should not take very long. Check the back of the stencil to see if there has been any bleeding of the paint. If so, make sure you clean the stencil before you move on to the next section.

9 Place your stencil in the next area for printing, lining up a section of the stencil over your previous print. Repeat steps 4–9 all over the whitewashed section of your piece of furniture. Whenever you run out of paint, load up and offload as before.

10 Use an artist's brush to top up any areas where the paint is too thin and to neaten any wobbly lines. When all the paint is completely dry, seal your finished table with a protective coat of clear, water-based varnish.

Well Rounded

This is a simple and effective way of adding arch shapes to your furniture, or even your walls, with a pop of colour. I love using the old-school method with a pencil and string to get the perfect curve. Alternatively, you may prefer to use household items such as plates or saucepan lids as templates. You can arrange your arches however you like and even overlap them.

TECHNIQUE: painting arches

MATERIALS

new furniture legs and screwdriver (optional)

electric sander and sanding block

primer

paintbrushes

satinwood paints, including white

pencil

pin

string

ruler

painter's tape

scissors

artist's brush

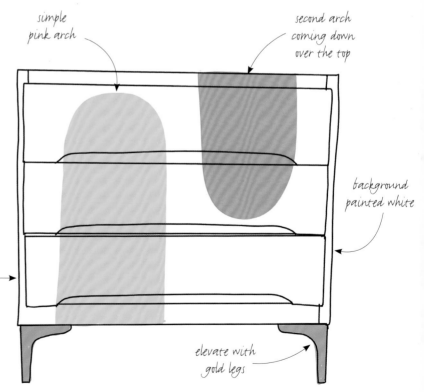

simple pink arch

second arch coming down over the top

background painted white

blue arch on the side

elevate with gold legs

1 Start by replacing the legs of your furniture piece, if desired, using a screwdriver – I added gold legs to this one. Prepare and prime the wooden surface as normal (see page 14) and then paint an all-over base coat of white satinwood.

2 Grab a pencil, a pin and a piece of string. Tie one end of the string to the pin and the other end to the pencil. Bear in mind that the length of the string will be the radius of the curve you are about to draw.

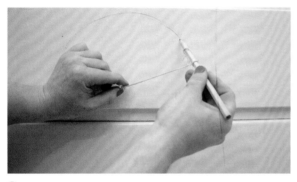

3 Place the pin on the painted wooden surface in the centre of where you want to draw the top of your arch. Keeping the string taut and the pencil straight, draw a semicircle shape.

4 Use your ruler to continue the pencil line straight down on both sides of the semicircle, as far as you want the arch to extend. You now have the outline of your first arch.

5 Use two straight pieces of painter's tape to mark out the sides of the arch. Take another piece of tape and cut a series of slits through ¾ of the width, leaving the last ¼ intact.

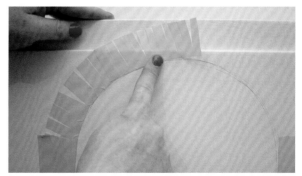

6 Follow the curved line of the arch with the piece of tape – the slits will allow the tape to bend into a curved line. Press it firmly into place all the way around.

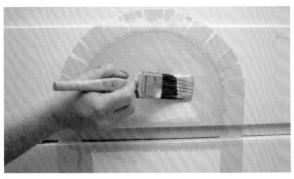

7 Paint your arch in a colour of your choice. If you want more control when painting the edges, use a small artist's brush so that the paint doesn't get too far onto the tape. Leave to dry, then add a second coat.

8 Without waiting for the final coat of paint to dry, slowly peel back the tape to reveal your arch. Repeat steps 2–8 to paint the remaining arches.

Transfer Day

This photocopy transfer technique offers endless possibilities, with a few limitations. The copy needs to be from a large photocopier or laser printer, not your home inkjet printer. You also have to apply the transfer to a porous surface that will absorb the ink, so this will not work on painted or varnished pieces, only bare wood. You will be using cellulose thinner to push the ink from the paper onto the surface, so read the product's safety guidelines before you begin. Work in a well-ventilated area and wear a mask and gloves.

TECHNIQUE: photocopy transfers

MATERIALS

screwdriver
wood filler and scraper (optional)
sanding block
photocopied images or illustrations
scissors
scrap wood for practice
painter's tape
mask and gloves
cellulose thinner and cotton pads
acrylic sealer or water-based varnish
paintbrushes
new handle (optional)
drill and drill bit (optional)
primer
satinwood paint

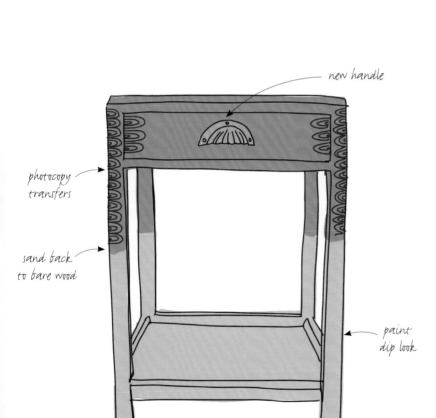

new handle

photocopy
transfers

sand back
to bare wood

paint
dip look

1 Before you begin, remove the hardware (if you are going to replace it later – see page 32) and sand the wooden surface thoroughly so that it is bare and free from any finish.

2 Cut out your photocopied design using scissors so that you have just the area you would like to transfer. You should have several copies so that you can practise the technique.

3 Start with a small piece of your design and a scrap of bare wood. Place the paper on the wood, printed side down, and secure it with painter's tape.

4 Wearing a mask and gloves in a well-ventilated area, soak a cotton pad with the cellulose thinner. Apply the thinner to the back of the paper, pressing down with a twisting motion.

5 You will begin to see that the paper is becoming transparent. Work your way around your design, using the same twisting motion as in step 4.

6 Peel back the paper to see how the design has transferred onto the wood. Repeat steps 4–6 to do a few test prints until you feel confident enough to start work on your furniture.

7 Cut out your design and put it in place, making sure the printed side is facing the wooden surface as before. Hold it in place with painter's tape.

8 Wearing gloves again, apply the thinner using a cotton pad as in step 4. If you are doing this on a vertical surface, you may find it easier to lay the piece down on the floor. Peel back the paper to reveal the print.

9 While the ink dries, repeat steps 7–9 on the next section of your piece of furniture until your design is complete. Leave to dry for a day or two and then apply a coat of acrylic sealer or water-based varnish to one of your test prints to make sure it doesn't lift the ink from the wood. You can then apply the sealer or varnish to your finished piece and replace the drawer handle, if desired (see page 32). Finally, use painter's tape, primer and satinwood paint to create a dipped paint effect on the legs (see page 28).

Pop and Block

I love the option of painting a section of a piece of furniture and leaving some of the wood visible. This table is made of dark wood, so I wanted to enhance it by using bright colours for contrast, and the sectional details gave me the idea to experiment with colour blocking. The base of the finished table looks like a tower of vibrantly hued Lego blocks, whereas the tabletop is dark and sleek. You can have the best of both worlds in one piece.

TECHNIQUE: colour blocking

MATERIALS

painter's tape
sanding block
primer
paintbrushes
satinwood paints
artist's brush
furniture reviver
furniture scratch cover

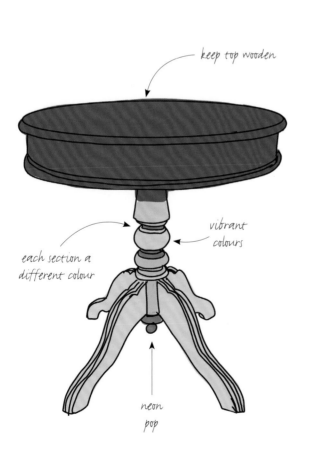

keep top wooden

vibrant
colours

each section a
different colour

neon
pop

1 Mark out the section where you are going to paint using painter's tape. Be careful to keep the line straight, especially if you are working on a curved surface. Prepare and prime the area you are going to paint (see page 14).

2 Decide which colour you want to use for each section of the table base and apply your first coat of paint. At this stage, don't worry too much if the colours overlap slightly.

3 Some areas can be difficult to reach when the table is upright, so you may need to turn it upside down to make it easier to paint everything. Leave to dry.

4 Build up the colour with a second layer of paint. You can overlap one colour onto the next and then, when it dries, paint over it to get a neat transition line.

5 Use an artist's brush to tidy up any lines that aren't straight. The small brush will give you much better control for a neater finish.

6 Remove the painter's tape after you have painted the final coat onto the uppermost section. You do not need to wait for the paint to dry before you do this.

7 When the paint is dry, use a furniture reviver to refresh the upper section of the table and bring out the natural grain of the wood. If there are any scratches, you can buff these out using a scratch cover solution in the same colour as the wood so that the table looks as good as new.

Flower Power

I love creating little templates out of paper when I want to apply a pattern to a piece of furniture. It's so easy to do and keeps everything looking uniform. Here, I used a simple daisy motif. You could do this in a more orderly, symmetrical way, and you could also put the flowers just on the drawer fronts, but I chose to scatter them all over the piece. It's more fun that way!

TECHNIQUE: all-over pattern

MATERIALS

Krud Kutter

screwdriver

new handles and legs with plate mounts (optional)

wood filler and scraper (optional)

drill and drill bit (optional)

electric sander and sanding block

primer

paintbrushes

eggshell or satinwood paints, including white and orange

pencil

paper

scissors

artist's brush

pattern all over top, sides and front

new gold drawer handles to look more luxurious

all-over daisy pattern to resemble wallpaper

mid-century-style wooden legs

1 This chest of drawers/dresser wasn't varnished, but it did have a little wax on the surface, so I cleaned it with Krud Kutter. Remove the old hardware from your chosen piece and then the furniture legs, if you are replacing them – this is easier if you turn the piece upside down.

2 Screw in the plate mounts for the replacement legs and twist the legs into place (see page 120), then turn the piece right-side up again. If you are replacing the drawer handles, fill and drill holes as needed (see page 32). Prepare and paint as normal (see page 14).

3 Use a pencil to draw or trace a simple daisy shape onto a piece of paper. Cut out the daisy – this will be your template.

4 Place the paper daisy template on the piece of furniture and draw around it with your pencil.

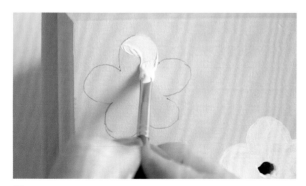

5 Scatter the daisies all over the piece or just on the drawer fronts. Fill in each daisy with white paint. This will take two coats, so allow the paint to dry after each coat.

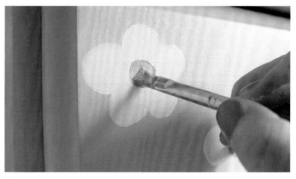

6 Take a small artist's brush and paint the centre of each of the daisies with orange paint – this is just a simple circle, so you should be able to do it freehand.

7 For awkward areas like the edges of the chest of drawers/dresser, you may need to bend the paper template as you draw around it. Once you have painted all the daisies, add the new handles (see page 32), or paint the old ones before putting them back, to give the piece a whole new look.

Between the Lines

This is a straightforward design that looks cool, graphic and edgy, especially on a piece with very straight lines such as this cupboard. Painter's tape will be your best friend here. It comes in a variety of widths, so you can have a bigger or smaller grid pattern if you like. I recommend using tape that is not fully opaque – this will allow you to see the lines you've already painted and keep everything straight.

TECHNIQUE: grid lines

MATERIALS

screwdriver
electric sander and sanding block
primer
paintbrushes
satinwood paint
neon paint
tape measure and ruler
pencil with eraser
painter's tape
artist's brush
spray paint (optional)
new hardware (optional)

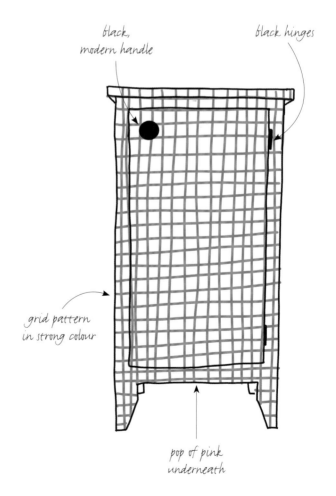

black, modern handle

black hinges

grid pattern in strong colour

pop of pink underneath

1 Remove the existing hardware (see page 32). Prepare, prime and paint the piece all over (see page 14) – I used white paint, with bright neon pink for the underside – then measure it and find the middle point on the top. Draw a pencil line from the front to the back, dividing the cupboard in half. Continue the line all the way down the front. This will be the starting point for the grid.

2 Place your painter's tape down the middle of the line you have drawn, all the way down the top and front of the cupboard, making sure you get into all the nooks and crannies. This is the first vertical line of your grid.

3 Working outwards from this central point, continue placing vertical strips of tape side by side all the way around the cupboard and on the top. Leave a little gap between each line of tape. Make sure the gaps are even in width, as this is where your painted grid lines will be. Press down each length of tape to ensure you get a crisp line.

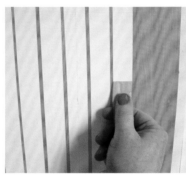

4 Paint all the vertical lines using neon paint in the colour of your choice. I chose the same bright pink that I had already used for the underside of the cupboard. It stands out really well against the white background.

5 Once you have finished painting, decide whether you need to apply a second coat. After the final coat, remove the tape straight away. Leave the paint to dry.

6 As in step 1, find the central starting point for the horizontal lines and mark it with the pencil, then cover it with tape. Add parallel lines of tape, leaving gaps between them of the same width as the vertical lines you have already painted.

7 Paint the horizontal lines, then remove the tape immediately (unless you need to apply a second coat) and leave the paint to dry.

8 Rub out the pencil lines with an eraser and tidy up any faint or uneven lines using an artist's brush. You can either spray paint the old hardware and then reattach it or replace it altogether (see page 32).

chapter 2

Intermediate Flips

On a Roll

Once you've got the hang of painting furniture, adding wallpaper is a really good way to bring in colour and pattern for a fun new look. Covering the front of these drawers with floral wallpaper had an immediate impact. You could also line the inside of the drawers for a nice little surprise when you open them. Before you begin, remove the drawers and lay them out in order, then write a number in chalk on the underside of each one so that you can put them back correctly later. If there are handles, remove them now.

TECHNIQUE: wallpapering

MATERIALS

chalk

screwdriver

electric sander and sanding block

primer

paintbrushes

good-quality wallpaper

satinwood paints

artist's brush

scissors

Mod Podge or wallpaper paste

dry sponge (optional)

craft blade

ruler (optional)

keep old handles

floral wallpaper

paint the drawer trim

satinwood paint

1 Prepare and prime the main body of the piece and the drawer fronts (see page 14). Put the drawers back in place and plan where you are going to put the wallpaper. The primer will prevent the wood from showing through. Paint the areas that will not be papered and leave to dry.

2 Make sure you have painted everything that will not be covered in wallpaper, including any small details. These drawers had a raised decorative trim that I decided to leave uncovered, so I painted this using an artist's brush. Leave to dry completely.

3 Take the drawers out again and line them up in order, with the drawer fronts facing upwards. Place a length of wallpaper over them and use your thumb and index finger to lightly crease the paper around the edge of each drawer front as a cutting guide.

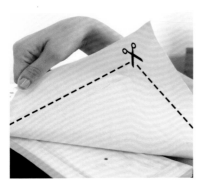

4 Cut around the crease line, not directly on the crease but leaving an extra bit of paper to make sure you have enough to cover each drawer completely. You can always cut any extra paper away later.

5 Check the wallpaper manufacturer's instructions. If they tell you to paste the paper, take a large brush and apply Mod Podge or wallpaper paste on the back of the paper in an even coat: not too thick, as this may cause bubbling, but enough to cover it. Set aside briefly to soak up the glue. However, if you are instructed to paste the wall, apply the Mod Podge or paste to the drawers.

6 Apply the paper to one drawer at a time. As you lay down the paper from left to right, continuously smooth it down with the palm of your hand and apply a little pressure to remove any air bubbles. This can also be done with a dry sponge. Smooth out the paper until the drawer front is covered. Repeat with the other drawers, then leave to dry.

7 With a sharp craft blade, carefully cut away the extra paper – you may find it helpful to use a ruler as a guide. Make very short cuts, as running the blade along the paper will cause it to rip.

8 Use the same method to cut around the drawer trim. Reattach the handles. To keep the paper from tearing when you do this, pierce small holes with the craft blade first. Finally, wipe off the chalk numbers and put the drawers back in place.

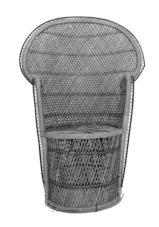

Wicker Wonder

A chair like this can be a real gem in any room. Wicker seats in all shapes and sizes are easy to find secondhand and are usually very comfortable to sit on. Painting wicker is not too difficult, but you will need to use spray paint instead of a brush. For an extra layer of protection, you can spray on a coat of varnish as well. I added some pale pink pompoms that match the colour of the paint and some yarn in a darker shade for contrast.

TECHNIQUE: spraying

MATERIALS

dry paintbrush

vacuum cleaner with brush attachment

mask

1 spray can of primer

2–3 spray cans of paint

hot glue gun and pompom trim (optional)

yarn and large sewing needle (optional)

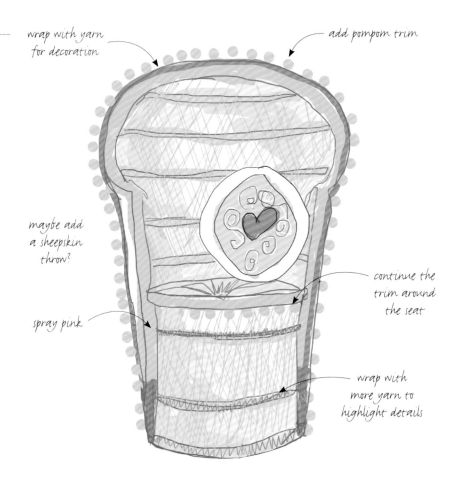

wrap with yarn for decoration

add pompom trim

maybe add a sheepskin throw?

spray pink

continue the trim around the seat

wrap with more yarn to highlight details

1 Wicker furniture always has to be cleaned thoroughly before it can be painted. Starting on the inside base of the chair, dry brush in the direction of the weave to dislodge all the built-up grime. Work your way around the chair.

2 Next, take your vacuum cleaner and use the brush attachment to remove all the dust. Once the chair is completely clean, it is ready to be sprayed.

3 Priming the wicker before you paint will make the colour more vibrant and the finish more durable. Shake the can of primer for at least five minutes before you break the seal.

4 While spraying, always wear a mask. Starting on the inside of the base, spray the chair with the primer. Move the spray can back and forth in fluid motions, slightly overlapping the previous area each time.

5 Work your way around the chair, making sure you have covered the entire surface. Leave the primer to dry completely before you start painting.

6 As in step 3, shake the can of paint for a full five minutes before you break the seal. Starting on the inside and wearing a mask, spray in the direction of the wicker weave so that everything is evenly covered. Don't overspray, as this will cause the paint to drip. Leave to dry.

7 When you apply the second coat, make sure you cover any areas that you missed. Leave to dry, then turn the chair upside down to check underneath. Spray again if needed.

8 If you like, you can decorate your chair with colourful yarn and other trimmings, especially if you want to hide any damaged areas. I used a hot glue gun to attach these pompoms.

9 You can also use a sewing needle to add some yarn in the colour(s) of your choice. Simply weave and wrap the yarn around the wicker until you have achieved the right look.

TECHNIQUE: typography

Just My Type

This is one of my favourite tricks. Carbon paper makes it really easy to transfer words and images onto the surface of your furniture – it's foolproof and saves so much time, like painting by numbers. Here, I created a simple typographic design with a drop shadow in a contrasting colour. Before you begin, remove any existing handles and fill in the holes left behind using wood filler (see page 32) so that you have a flat surface to work on.

MATERIALS

screwdriver
wood filler and scraper
sanding block and electric sander
clear, water-based varnish
primer
paintbrushes
satinwood paints
painter's tape
printed letters
carbon paper
pencil
artist's brushes
new handles (optional)
drill and drill bit (optional)

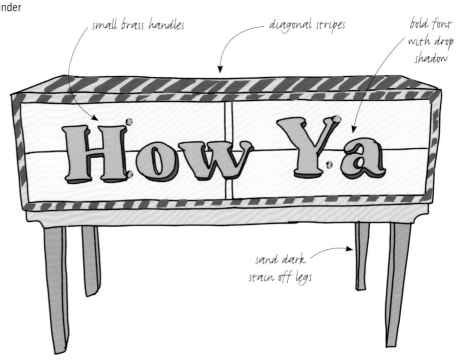

small brass handles

diagonal stripes

bold font with drop shadow

sand dark stain off legs

1 Sand the legs and add a coat of clear, water-based varnish (see page 21), then leave to dry. Prepare and prime everything else (see page 14) and apply a base coat of paint. For the diagonal stripes, I used painter's tape 5cm/2in wide. To keep the spacing even, I used a small piece of tape as a guide.

2 Make sure that the tape is secure and paint the diagonal lines in a contrasting colour. Add a second coat if you need to. Remove the tape as soon as you have full coverage and then wait for the paint to dry.

3 Your lettering should be printed out at full size – you may need several sheets of paper. I made sure to include the drop shadow. Tape each of the letters in position, making sure everything lines up correctly.

4 Place the carbon paper behind your first letter with the darker side facing the painted surface. With a sharp pencil, trace over the outline of the letter and its shadow.

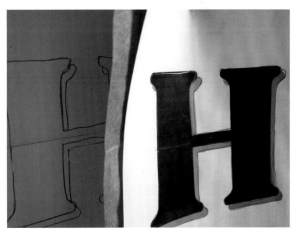

5 The outline will be transferred onto the piece of furniture. Move the carbon paper to the next letter and repeat step 4 until you have traced the whole of your design.

6 Using an artist's brush, paint the letters in your chosen colour. You may need to apply two coats. Leave to dry completely.

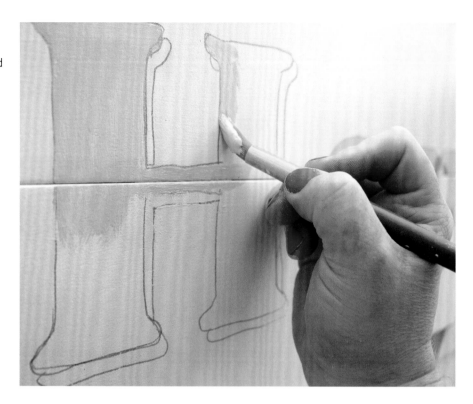

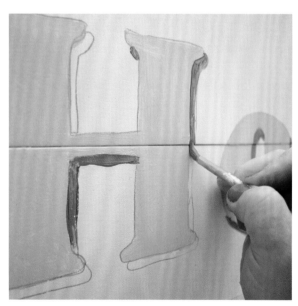

7 With a thinner brush, paint the drop shadow in a different colour. Again, you may need two coats. Leave to dry.

8 Touch up the edges of the letters with more paint as needed so that all the lines are neat and crisp. Leave to dry.

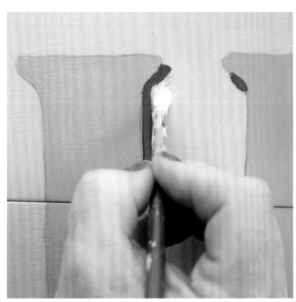

9 Paint around the edges of the letters using your base colour as well. This will take a little time, but it will make a big difference in the end. Leave to dry.

10 Finally, if you would like to add new handles or other hardware, you can do this now (see page 32). I chose these small brass handles, which don't compete with the lettering.

Panel Show

A classic sideboard/credenza looks really impressive in a hallway or dining room. It can even be used as a dressing table/vanity if you have the space. This one had been painted previously, but not very well, so it needed to be stripped back. There was also some damage to the veneer on the doors and drawer fronts. However, I couldn't resist the curved doors, so I decided to cover the imperfections with panelling and replace the handles with a more modern design.

TECHNIQUE: panelling

MATERIALS

screwdriver

electric sander with sponge attachment and sanding block

measuring tape and pencil

3cm/1¼in-wide wooden slats

saw and mitre box

No More Nails glue

hammer and tack nails

primer

wood filler

dampened cloth

paintbrushes

satinwood paint

terrazzo handles (optional)

drill and drill bit (optional)

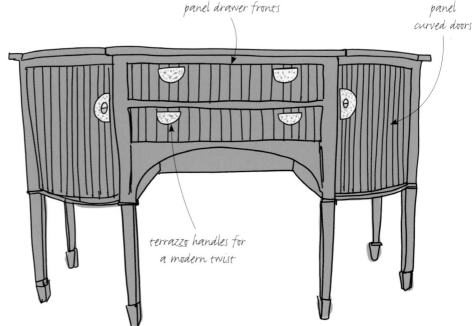

panel drawer fronts

panel curved doors

terrazzo handles for a modern twist

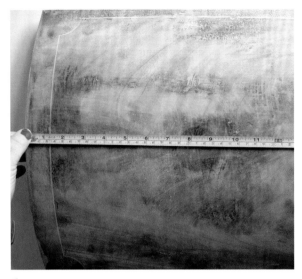

1 Remove the hardware and prepare the surface of the wood (see page 14). Take the curved doors off their hinges – this will make them a lot easier to work on. Measure the height of one of the doors to work out how long the panels should be.

2 Measure the first slat and mark the length you need with a pencil. You will need to measure and cut one piece at a time – don't mark out multiple pieces before cutting, as the thickness of the saw can slightly alter the length of the panel.

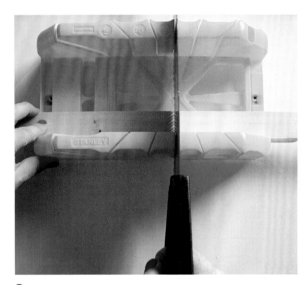

3 Using a mitre box for accuracy, place the panel against the inner edge of the box to keep it straight. Cut your first panel and make sure it is the correct length, then measure and cut the rest. Place them on the door to check the spacing. If you are left with a gap at one end, you can leave a small space in between each panel so that the door is fully covered.

4 Take the No More Nails glue and apply it to the back of the first panel, then place it in the centre of the door and press it down so that the glue spreads out evenly. Do not use regular wood glue, as it will not be able to hold the panels in position on the curved surface for long enough to let the glue dry. No More Nails dries quickly, so the panels will remain in place.

5 Working outward from the centre, glue all the panels onto the door, making sure each one is correctly aligned and that the spacing between the panels is even.

6 Hammer in some tack nails to hold the panels in place as the glue dries. You don't need to nail down every single one, just a few of them. Leave to dry for 24 hours. Meanwhile, repeat steps 2–6 for the other door.

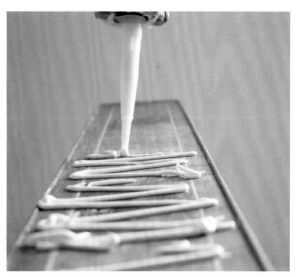

7 Measure the height of each drawer front, taking into account any decorative trim around the edge. You want the panels to cover the drawers completely.

8 Repeat steps 2–3 to measure and cut out the panels for the first drawer front. Place them down without glue first to check the spacing, then remove them and apply No More Nails glue to the drawer.

9 Starting in the centre of the drawer, glue down the first panel and then work your way outward to glue the rest.

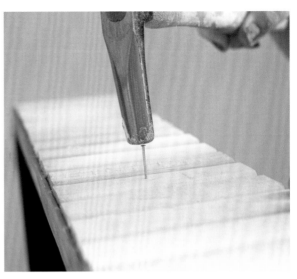

10 Hammer in some tack nails as before and leave the glue to dry for 24 hours. Meanwhile, repeat steps 8–10 for the other drawer fronts so that all the panelling is in place.

11 Fit a sponge attachment to your electric sander and tilt the sander to get a nice bevel on each end of the panels. Brush off any dust from sanding.

12 Reattach the doors and put the drawers back into place, unless you would prefer to do this later, then prime the entire piece. Priming before using wood filler can make it easier to spot the areas that need to be filled.

13 Apply wood filler to the ends of the panelling, the nail holes and the gaps in between each slat. This will smooth out any imperfections before you start painting.

14 With a lightly dampened cloth, wipe away any excess wood filler – this will make sanding easier. Leave the filler to dry completely.

15 Sand back all the areas you filled with a sanding block until smooth and then remove the dust as before.

16 Paint the piece and reassemble it, if you haven't already. I added new terrazzo handles (see page 32), but you could reattach the original hardware if you prefer.

Geometry Lesson

This project will need a little extra time, but trust me, it will be worth it. After you have prepared and primed your piece, make a quick sketch to plan your overall geometric look, as in the example below. Think about your palette and decide on the approximate size of the triangles you want to paint. You could use a ruler and be very precise, but in my view that takes all the fun out of it. I also decided to remove the mirrored panel from this piece and paint the interior.

After your first set of triangles is complete, use them as the basis for your next set. There may be some larger triangles and some smaller ones, but that's OK: it will all come together in the end. Make sure you use Frog Tape for marking out the triangles, as it's better than regular painter's tape for this kind of project.

TECHNIQUE: geometric shapes

MATERIALS

screwdriver
wood filler and scraper
sanding block and electric sander
primer
paintbrushes
sketchpad and coloured pencils
satinwood paints
Frog Tape
new handles (optional)
drill and drill bit (optional)

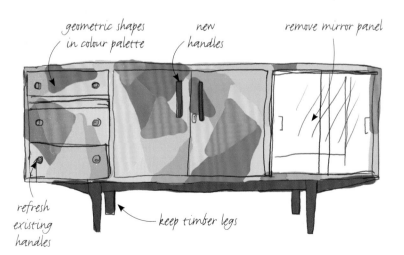

geometric shapes in colour palette

new handles

remove mirror panel

refresh existing handles

keep timber legs

1 Remove any existing hardware and fill any holes left behind, then prepare the wood surface and apply a coat of primer (see page 14). Sketch out your plan, then mark out the first layer of triangles with Frog Tape. Press it down firmly.

2 Now it is time to start painting your triangles. Don't apply the paint too heavily, or you will be left with thick lines of dried paint at the edges. Peel back the tape, then leave the paint to dry completely before you continue.

3 Once the first layer of paint is completely dry, use more tape to mark out the next layer of triangular shapes over the edges of the dry ones.

4 Paint the second layer of triangles in the colour of your choice, as in step 2. Peel back the tape, then leave until the paint is fully dry.

5 Repeat steps 3–4 to add further layers of triangular shapes in different colours until the area you want to paint is completely covered. Gently peel back the Frog Tape in between each layer, immediately after you have finished painting. After I painted this piece, I also replaced the two handles on the central doors with new ones, which I installed in a different position (see page 32).

Time for a Change

I love the idea of transforming something old and unwanted, making it fit my personal style but also keeping it functional. Turning this grandfather clock digital has given it a stylish, modern twist while still honouring its original purpose. Using paint markers really saves on time when you have to do those finer details – you can buy empty ones and fill them with paint in any colour you like. Before you start painting, I recommend making a sketch like the one below as a guide.

TECHNIQUE: paint pens

MATERIALS

screwdriver and screws

electric sander and sanding block

primer

paintbrushes

sketchpad and coloured pencils

satinwood paints

artist's brushes

measuring jug/cup

Owatrol paint conditioner

empty paint marker

cardboard

pencil (optional)

battery-powered digital
    clock face

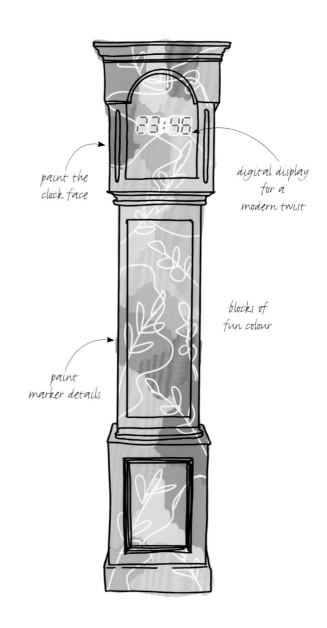

paint the
clock face

digital display
for a
modern twist

blocks of
fun colour

paint
marker details

1 Remove the clock face – on this clock it was attached with screws at the back. Take off the hands and dismantle the mechanism. If you would like to reuse it, store all the parts carefully.

2 Prepare and prime the face and body of the clock (see page 14), then leave to dry. Sketch out your plan, then start applying large, freehand blocks of colour all over the clock.

3 Where two colours meet, try not to leave any gaps, but be careful to make sure the shades don't mix together. Apply two coats of each colour, leaving the paint to dry after each one.

4 Use a flat artist's brush to tidy up the edges of each colour block. The lines don't need to be straight, but the edges should be sharp. As in step 3, try not to mix the different colours. Leave to dry.

5 For the paint marker, mix one part Owatrol paint conditioner to one part paint in a measuring jug/cup. Open the empty marker and pour the mixture inside, then secure the lid. Pump the marker so that the paint soaks into the nib. Test it on a scrap piece of cardboard to make sure the paint is flowing nicely.

6 Reattach the clock face and draw your design onto the clock using the marker. If you like, you can draw a light pencil line first as a guide and then use the marker to trace over it. Leave to dry.

7 Affix a screw to the clock face and hang the battery-operated digital clock. Make sure the paint marker lines go right up to the new display.

8 You may need to apply a second coat with the marker in certain areas, especially if you are using white paint on top of darker colours. When the final coat is dry, your clock is finished.

Raise the Bar

I flipped this drinks cabinet using a combination of several different painting techniques for a unique finish. I love how bright and colourful it is. For an optional extra, you could line the drawers with patterned wallpaper for a nice little surprise when you open them (see page 62). As with the grandfather clock project (see page 86), I recommend making a sketch like the one below before you begin.

TECHNIQUE: freehand painting

MATERIALS

electric sander and sanding block
primer
paintbrushes
sketchpad and coloured pencils
eggshell and satinwood paints
artist's brushes
Frog Tape
pencil with eraser
ruler (optional)
cardboard
scissors
vinyl decals
spray paint (optional)

spray old handles

polka dots

vinyl decals

continue pattern all the way around

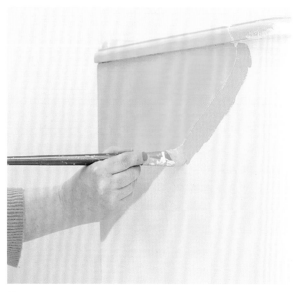

1 Remove the handles. After preparing and priming (see page 14), sketch out your plan and map out the placement of the freehand colour blocks on your piece. Paint the outlines first, then fill in the colour blocks. This is only the first coat, so don't worry if they aren't perfect. Leave to dry.

2 Now it is time to go over the shapes you have painted. On this second coat, concentrate on getting a crisp line in between the different colours – I recommend using a flat artist's brush for the edges. Leave to dry.

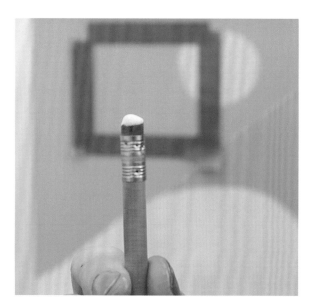

3 Mark out a square section using Frog Tape. This can overlap multiple colour blocks if you like. Next, take your pencil and dip the eraser in a little bit of paint. This will allow you to create small polka dots within the square of tape.

4 Starting in the middle of the square, create a horizontal line of polka dots. Repeat this process, but stagger the placement of the dots in each row as seen in this photograph. You can use a ruler to measure the spacing if you like, or just do it by eye. Remove the tape without waiting for the paint to dry.

5 Freestyle some circles using an artist's brush – I used satinwood paint for this. You will need to apply two coats, but make sure you leave the paint to dry in between.

6 To make a quick stencil, draw a rough circle shape onto a piece of cardboard and then cut it out with scissors. Secure the stencil in place with Frog Tape and then paint a series of thin vertical lines over it using a small artist's brush.

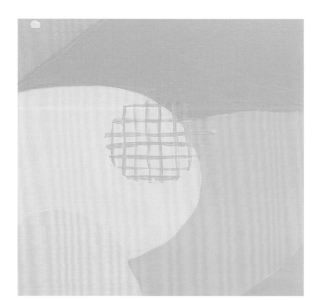

7 Paint more lines over the stencil, but this time paint them in a horizontal direction to make a criss-cross pattern. Remove the stencil without waiting for the paint to dry.

8 Next, use Frog Tape to mark out some straight lines, as above. Paint the lines using satinwood paint, then peel back the tape and leave to dry.

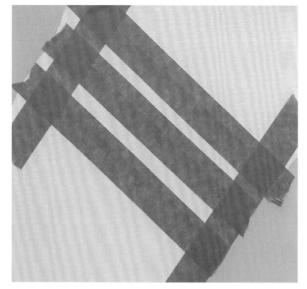

9 You can then add more of these lines in between the ones you painted before. This time, place the Frog Tape over the first set of lines, then paint the second set as before.

10 Peel back the tape to reveal the closely spaced parallel lines, then leave to dry completely.

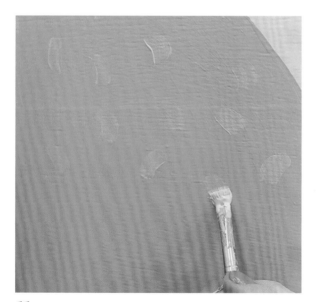

11 To create a confetti-style pattern, choose a small area of the piece and use a small, flat artist's brush to paint short curved lines in different directions.

12 For a simple finishing touch, choose a few small vinyl decals to add to the piece. Stick them on and then rub them firmly to make sure they stay in place. Spray paint the handles if you like, then reattach them.

Swatch This!

Inspiration can come from many different places, even from a paint chart. I love seeing a palette of colours in vibrant shades and variations all in one place, so why not recreate the look on a piece of furniture? This project is not too difficult, but it needs patience, planning and a lot of mixing.

TECHNIQUE: mixing colours

MATERIALS

electric sander and sanding block

primer

paintbrushes

satinwood paints, including white

artist's brushes

circle template (this can be any small, round object)

pencil

colour mixing palettes

clingfilm/plastic wrap

new handles (optional)

drill and drill bit (optional)

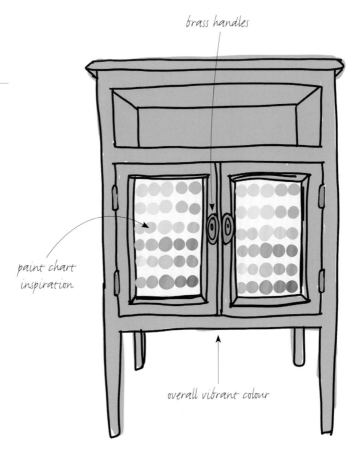

brass handles

paint chart inspiration

overall vibrant colour

1 After preparing and priming (see page 14), decide where your colour swatches are going to go and paint these areas white. Paint the rest of your piece in a colour of your choice, using an artist's brush around the edges of the white areas for greater control.

2 Take a round object the same size as the circles you want to draw and plan out how many rows you can fit in the white areas of your piece and how many circles on each row. Draw around the object with a pencil to create as many circles as you need.

3 Each row of swatches will be based on one colour of paint, with the most intense shade on the left and the palest on the right. Put your first colour in one section of a mixing palette and paint the left-most circle in the first row.

4 In another section of the palette, mix the same colour with a small amount of white. For the next shade, add more white. Repeat until the number of shades is the same as the number of swatches in the row, then paint one circle in each shade. Cover the palette in clingfilm/plastic wrap and set aside.

5 Take a fresh mixing palette and repeat steps 3 and 4 for the next line of colours, working your way from the darkest shade to the lightest. Leave to dry.

6 Use a small artist's brush and some white paint to sharpen the outlines of the circles. Some of the colour swatches may need a little topping up as well – the clingfilm/plastic wrap will keep the paint wet in case you need to go back in and reapply any of your custom shades. Leave to dry, then attach new handles if you like (see page 32).

Sew Stylish

The cane backing on this chair made the perfect blank canvas for a giant cross stitch design. This technique is a great way to add colour and personality to a vintage piece without any commitment to a permanent change, as the stitches can be easily removed. A little extra care is needed to make sure that the back is as neat as the front – remember that both sides will be visible.

TECHNIQUE: cross stitch

MATERIALS

sanding block
graph paper
coloured pencils
yarn
large sewing needle
scissors
paper and pencil (optional)
clear, water-based varnish
paintbrush
painter's tape (optional)
satinwood paint
artist's brush

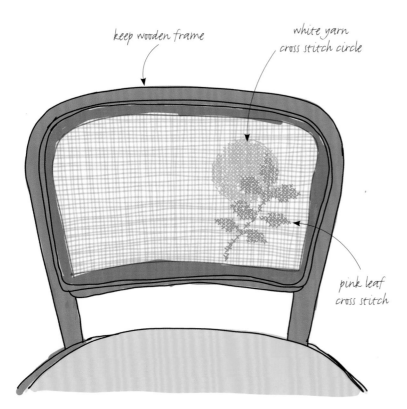

keep wooden frame

white yarn
cross stitch circle

pink leaf
cross stitch

1 Sand back the finish on the chair frame. I did this by hand using a sanding block, which was more time consuming than using an electric sander but prevented any damage to the rounded shape of the wood. Make sure the chair is free of dust, especially the cane.

2 Take a piece of graph paper and plan out your cross stitch design using coloured pencils that match the hues of your yarn. You will need this plan to refer to as you make your stitches.

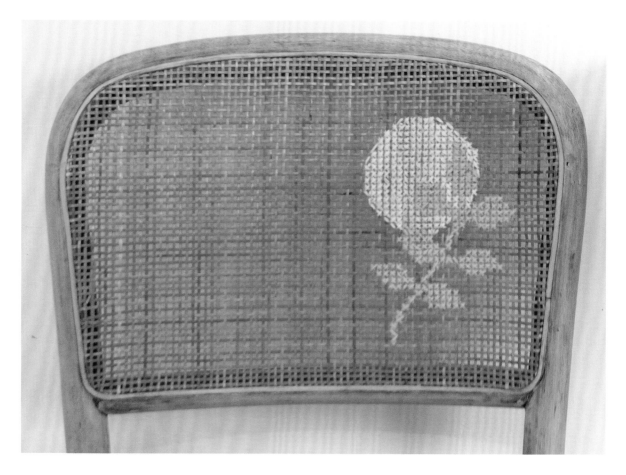

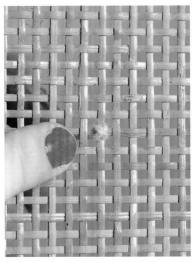

3 Thread a sewing needle with yarn and begin your first stitch. Hold the end of the yarn in place at the back of the chair – you can tuck this in later. Pass the needle back through the weave to make a diagonal stitch.

4 With your second stitch, cross the yarn back over in the opposite diagonal to create your first cross stitch. It should look like a little 'X'.

5 Keep following your sketch and add more stitches – I began with a vertical line to make a stem for my leaf design.

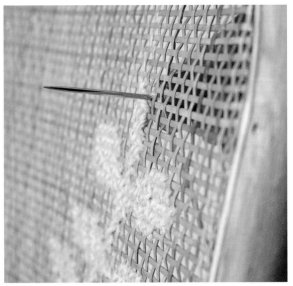

6 Continue stitching and see how your design takes shape. The sketch is only a guide, so you can change the size and shape of the leaves if you need to.

7 When you have completed all the stitches in one colour, trim the yarn, leaving a short tail. Tuck this into the previous stitch to prevent it from unravelling.

8 If your design includes a circle shape, you may want to make a paper template to use as a guide. Hold the template against the back of the chair to check the size and position of the cross stitch circle.

9 With a lighter-coloured yarn, cross stitch the circle – you may only need to make one diagonal stitch in places where you are following the curved outline. If you have a template, hold it up every now and then to ensure your circle looks OK.

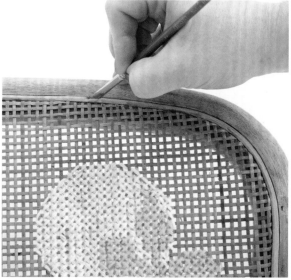

10 Continue stitching your way around the circle, filling in all the spaces between the leaves. When you have finished stitching, trim the yarn and tuck in the end, as in step 7.

11 Seal the frame with a clear, water-based varnish all over, or if you like, you can create a dipped paint look using painter's tape (see page 28). Finally, use an artist's brush to paint the edge of the cane to match one of the yarn colours.

chapter 3

Advanced Flips

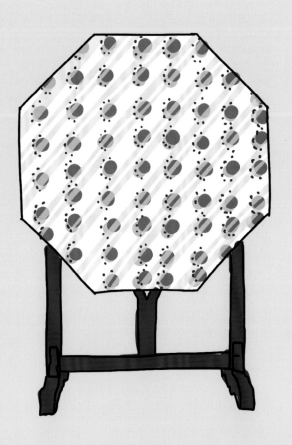

Stores Galore

A bespoke, built-in pantry can be very costly to install, but there is a much more affordable solution: converting an old wardrobe/ armoire into a freestanding pantry cupboard. These vintage designs have lots of character. They also tend to be less deep than their modern counterparts, which is great for a pantry because items will be less likely to get lost at the back. The finished piece with its decorative cane panels would also make a wonderful linen closet.

TECHNIQUE: cane panelling

MATERIALS

screwdriver

ruler, tape measure and spirit level

wood filler and scraper

sanding block and electric sander

primer

paintbrushes

satinwood paints

wallpaper and paste (optional)

saw and mitre box

lengths of wood with a 1.2cm/½in square cross section

cane webbing and scissors

staple gun and staples

hammer and nails

No More Nails glue

lengths of wood with a 4.5cm x 2cm/ 1¾in x ¾in cross section

MDF or plywood boards

wooden scalloped trim (optional)

new hardware and label holders (optional)

drill and drill bit (optional)

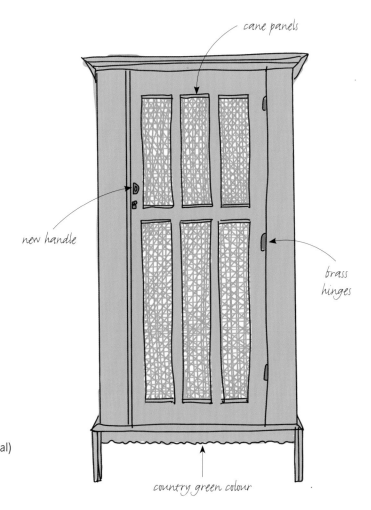

cane panels

new handle

brass hinges

country green colour

1 Take the door off its hinges and remove the backing from each wooden panel using a ruler. Take out the panels and set them aside for later.

2 Remove any existing hardware (such as hooks or rails) from the interior. Fill in the holes with wood filler. I also filled in the carved details at the top of the door, but this is optional. Scrape off any excess filler and leave to dry, then sand until smooth (see page 32).

3 Prepare, prime and paint the inside and outside of the piece (see page 14), or alternatively you can wallpaper the inside (see page 62). Prepare, prime and paint the door as well, then leave to dry completely.

4 Use a saw and mitre box to cut down the original wooden panels by 1.2cm/½in all the way around. Make a frame around each panel out of lengths of wood with a 1.2cm/½in square cross section. Glue each frame together with No More Nails, but don't glue the panels into the frames. When the glue is dry, remove the panels and set them aside for later, then prime and paint the frames to match the door.

5 Take a pair of scissors and cut a piece of cane webbing for each panel – these should be slightly larger than the openings in the door. The cane needs to be soaked before it can be applied, so fill a sink with cold water, add the webbing pieces and leave for 20 minutes.

6 If you stretch the webbing onto the frames now, the tension will cause the wood to warp. To prevent this, take the original wooden panels that you cut down in step 4 and put them back inside the frames while you work. After the cane has soaked for 20 minutes, stretch each piece of webbing onto its frame and fix in place with a staple gun. Then leave to dry completely with the wooden panels still in place.

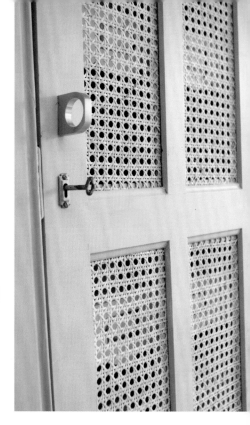

7 Once the cane is dry and the webbing is nice and taut on the frames, pop out the wooden panels and cut off the excess webbing around the edges.

8 Apply No More Nails glue around the inside of the door panel openings and pop in the webbing panels.

9 Fix the frames in position by hammering nails into the door frame. Leave the glue to dry for 24 hours. In the meantime, you can start work on the shelves for your new pantry.

FOR THE SHELVES

10 Measure the width of the pantry's interior and use a saw and mitre box to cut lengths of 4.5cm x 2cm/1¾ x ¾in wood, one to support each shelf.

11 Glue the back of one of these wooden brackets and place it just below where you want the first shelf to sit. Hammer a nail into the centre to hold it in place.

12 With a spirit level, make sure that the bracket is perfectly horizontal and hammer in a nail at either end to hold it in position. Repeat steps 11 and 12 for the other brackets.

13 Next, measure the depth of the interior and cut two side brackets for each shelf. Repeat steps 11 and 12 to fix these in place. Fill the nail holes with wood filler as in step 2. After sanding back the filler, prime and paint all the brackets. Leave to dry.

14 Cut up your MDF or plywood boards to make shelves – some hardware stores will cut them to size for you. Prime the shelves and leave to dry, then place them in position and add a little glue and nails to secure them. Add the scalloped trim (if using), then paint the shelves and leave to dry.

15 I loved the old hooks and hangers, so I cleaned these and fixed them back into position. I also added a new brass handle and hinges to the door and some metal label holders to the shelf trims (see page 32). Put the door back on the wardrobe – you might need an extra pair of hands to help you.

Table Talk

Herringbone is a timeless pattern, and so beautiful in any kind of wood. Paint stir sticks are a great, budget-friendly way to create a herringbone pattern that will enhance an old piece of furniture. They are widely available, inexpensive to buy and very easy to cut. Because the sticks are made of wood, you can stain them in any colour to suit your style or simply seal them with varnish.

TECHNIQUE: pattern

MATERIALS

electric sander
paint stir sticks
saw and mitre box
ruler and tape measure
pencil
painter's tape
No More Nails glue
wood filler
120 grit sandpaper
primer
paintbrushes
satinwood paint
clear, water-based varnish

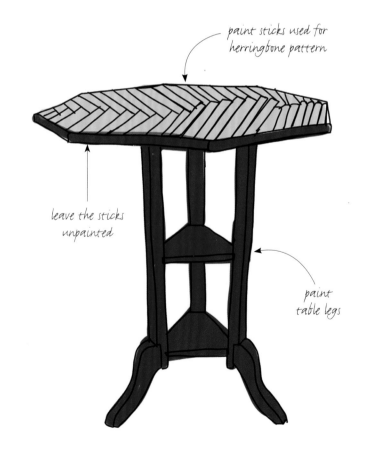

paint sticks used for herringbone pattern

leave the sticks unpainted

paint table legs

1 Sand back the top of the table to remove any existing paint, wood stain or varnish. The stir sticks will adhere much better to this bare surface.

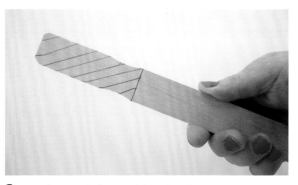

2 Saw off the end of each stick so that there are no curved edges, using a mitre box for safety and accuracy – you may want to draw a line across each one using a ruler and pencil to mark where you should cut.

3 Measure the exact middle of the table and put down a strip of painter's tape so that one edge runs along this central line. This will act as a guide to help you arrange your first row of sticks for the herringbone pattern.

4 Place the sticks down without any glue at first so that you can get an idea of how you will lay them out and what the pattern is going to look like. Use the tape as a marker of where one corner of each stick in the first row should be.

5 When you are happy with the layout, add No More Nails glue to each stick, one at a time. Fix the first stick firmly in place on the table, pressing down so that the wood is level and the excess glue spreads out evenly. Repeat with the rest of the sticks in the first row, then peel off the tape.

6 Apply some more glue to the central area of the table, where the tape used to be, and add a second row of stir sticks – they should interlock with the first row to form a herringbone pattern. Repeat until the table is mostly covered, except for the edges.

7 The edge pieces will have to be cut to size before being glued down. Place a stir stick in position and draw a line with a ruler and pencil to mark where the edge of the table will be. Cut along the line, then glue the stick in place and repeat until the table is fully covered. Leave to dry for 24 hours.

8 Fill in all the gaps in between the sticks using wood filler and leave to dry overnight. Don't worry if it looks messy, as the excess filler will be sanded away later.

9 Sand the surface back with 120 grit sandpaper, then sand back the edges of the table as well. Prime and paint the base of the table, including the edges. Seal the herringbone tabletop with a coat of clear, water-based varnish.

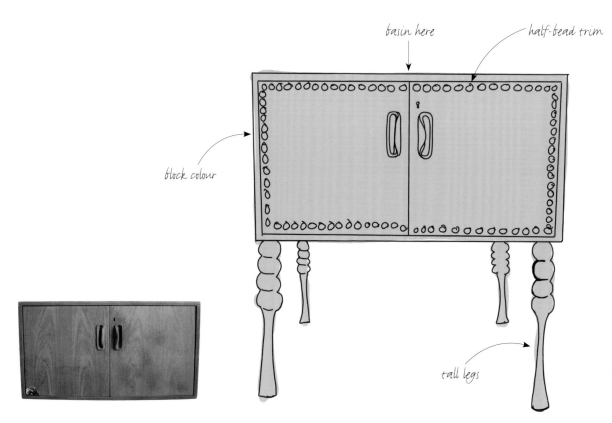

basin here

half-bead trim

block colour

tall legs

MATERIALS

screwdriver
electric sander and sanding block
half wooden beads
No More Nails glue
primer
paintbrushes
satinwood paint
artist's brush
new furniture legs with plate mounts
drill and drill bit (optional)
basin

Make a Splash

A bathroom vanity is a great opportunity to make a design statement. I made this one by adding legs to a basic cabinet to bring it up to the perfect height. A plumber will be able to help you install a basin and hook it up to the water supply. This will involve drilling a plughole/drain into the top of your vanity and making a space for the pipes to come in at the back, but a professional will be able to advise you on creating the best setup for your home.

1 Remove the doors from their hinges so that you have a flat surface on which to arrange the beads before you glue them down. Prepare the wooden surface of the cabinet and doors for painting (see page 14).

2 Place the beads around the edges of the doors. Do this without glue first so that you can play around with the layout and spacing before making a final decision.

3 Pick up one of the beads, dab a little No More Nails glue on the back and fix it in place, pressing down firmly.

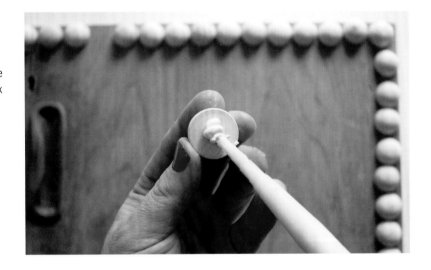

4 Repeat with the other beads, working your way around the edges of both doors. Leave to dry for at least 24 hours so that everything is secure.

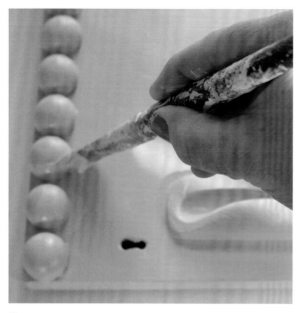

5 Prime and paint the doors. Use an artist's brush for the half-bead trim and any other awkward areas. Prime and paint the main body of the piece as well. Leave everything to dry.

6 Before you attach the legs, turn the unit upside down. Use a screwdriver to affix the plate mounts onto the base, one in each corner. Some legs have an additional screw attached, for which you will need to drill a hole.

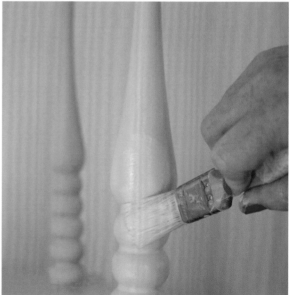

7 Attach the legs to the mounts by twisting them into the plate so that they are securely fixed in place.

8 Prime and paint the legs. When the final coat is dry, flip the vanity back the right way up and reattach the doors. Your vanity is now ready to have a basin installed by a plumber.

Layers Upon Layers

Stencils come in all different shapes, sizes and styles. With a few tricks, they are easy to use and look great on furniture, walls and floors. Even a single stencil can be used to create a layered design if you play around with colour. If you have a few stencils to choose from, you can layer the different shapes and colours on top of one another. This cute little folding table was the perfect example of this kind of project. Always remember to upload your brush with paint and then offload the excess before you stencil.

TECHNIQUE: layering stencils

MATERIALS

screwdriver (optional)
electric sander and sanding block
primer
paintbrushes
satinwood paints
cardboard
stencil brush
set of stencils
Frog Tape
artist's brush
wallpaper and paste (optional)

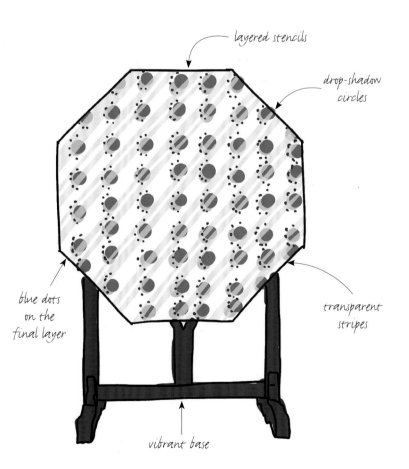

layered stencils

drop-shadow circles

blue dots on the final layer

transparent stripes

vibrant base

1 Before I started, I removed the top of the table so it would be easier to work on, but this is optional. Prepare and prime the table (see page 14). Paint the base in the colour of your choice, then paint the top in a light colour. Leave to dry.

2 Set up your tools for stencilling. You will need a scrap of cardboard, a stencil brush – this is a special type of paintbrush with short, tightly packed bristles – and a set of stencils. I began with this polka dot design.

3 Place the stencil in the middle of your piece and fix it in position using Frog Tape so that it doesn't move around while you are working.

4 Upload your stencil brush with paint in the colour you have chosen for the first layer. Keep your brush upright and make sure you don't add too much paint.

5 Offload some of the paint on the scrap of cardboard. You may think that you don't have enough paint left on your brush after doing this, but trust me – less is more.

6 Keep the stencil brush upright and buff in circular motions until the area inside the circle is covered in paint. Peel back the tape and check the back of the stencil – if any paint has seeped underneath, the stencil will need to be washed and dried before you continue.

7 Tape down the stencil in a new position, but keep it lined up with the circles you painted in step 6. Some stencils have marks to help with this, or you can overlap the design. Repeat steps 4–7 until the first layer is complete, then leave to dry. In the meantime, wash and dry your stencil.

8 To create a drop shadow on your next layer, just drop the stencil slightly down and to the right of the first layer and tape it down, then repeat steps 4–7. A darker colour than your first layer works best for this. Leave the second layer of paint to dry as before.

9 For the next layer, I added some stripes with Frog Tape. This is optional. Apply the Frog Tape in diagonal lines, leaving a 1cm/½in gap in between each line of tape. Paint the stripes using a light colour – this will allow the darker colours underneath to show through for a translucent effect.

10 As soon as you have finished painting the stripes, peel the tape off. Leave this third layer of paint to dry completely before you move on to the fourth and final layer.

11 Line up the final stencil with the existing circles, tape it in place and repeat steps 4–7, remembering to upload and offload as before. If your stencil has lots of small details like these little circles, paint them one at a time and keep the brush upright throughout. Remove the stencil and leave the paint to dry completely.

12 With a small artist's brush, tidy up the paintwork where needed so that all the lines are crisp and clear, then leave to dry. If you like, add some wallpaper to the underneath of the table (see page 62). Then, if you removed the tabletop from the base in step 1, it is time to reassemble everything.

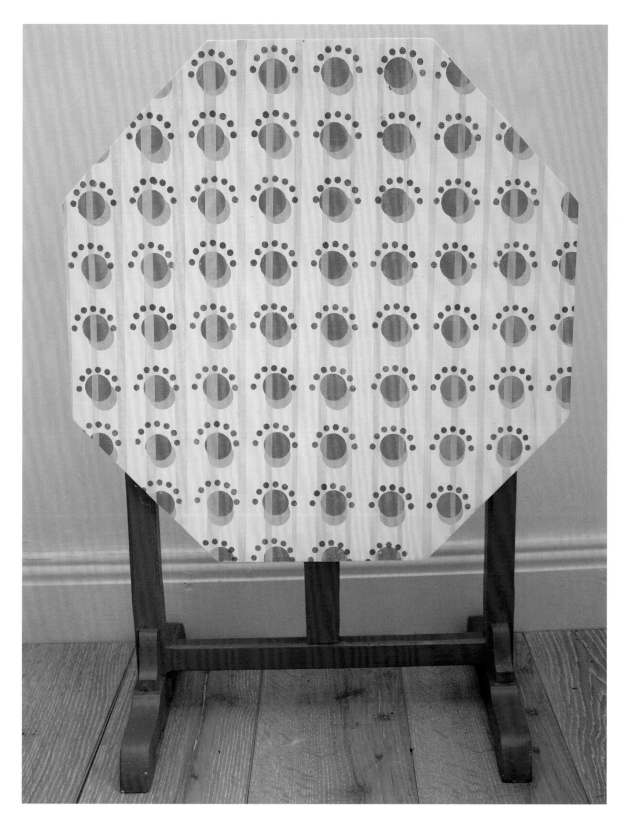

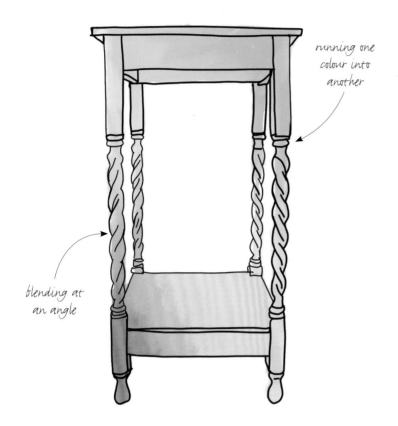

running one
colour into
another

blending at
an angle

Colour Cloud

Blending colours can give such a nice effect, whether you use different shades of the same hue or a full spectrum. You may not have used paint conditioner before, but for this project it will be your best friend. When you add it to satinwood paint, it slows down the drying time, which allows you to perfect the blend. It also gives the paint a smoother finish, among other benefits.

TECHNIQUE: colour blending

MATERIALS

sanding block

primer

paintbrushes

satinwood paints, including white

6 small jars

Owatrol paint conditioner

paint stir sticks

large round brush for blending

1 Prime your piece of furniture as normal, then apply a coat of white satinwood paint all over. This is going to allow you to concentrate just on blending the colours and not worry about getting coverage on your first coat of paint. Leave to dry.

2 You are going to apply the different paint colours freehand in diagonal sections, starting in the lower left and right corners. Paint the first section in the lower left – I used a bright shade of pink.

3 Paint the second and third colours – I used yellow and pale pink – in the next two diagonal sections. Where two colours meet, lightly start to blend them together, but don't go too far. You can blend them more thoroughly on the final coat.

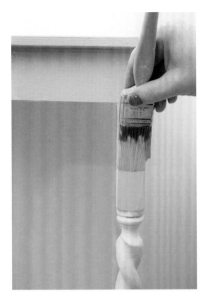

4 Go to the upper right-hand corner now. Take your fourth colour – I used pale aqua – and paint a new diagonal section as in step 2, but this time working down and to the left.

5 Paint your fifth colour in the last diagonal section – I used pale blue. Lightly blend it with the fourth colour but not the third, leaving some white space in the middle. Leave to dry.

6 Take a small jar for each of your five colours and another for the white. In each jar, combine three parts paint to one part paint conditioner, mixing well with a paint stir stick. This will allow the paint to flow better.

7 Starting with the jar containing the first colour you used, take a large round brush and buff in the paint where the first two colours meet. Feather the brush in the same direction to blend the colours so that there is no longer a distinct line between them. You can add a little of the second colour if you need to blend them further. Keep standing back from the piece so that you can tell which area may need a little extra buffing. Repeat with the other jars of paint until everything is nicely blended. When you are satisfied, leave to fully dry.

Cube Illusion

I love the 3D effect that this trompe l'oeil cube pattern brings. It can be a little tricky to accomplish, but after you get your first cube done, the process speeds up. It is much easier to create this kind of design on a flat surface, such as a cupboard door – simply remove it from its hinges before you begin. This isn't a project you can complete in a single day, but the finished look is worth the effort.

TECHNIQUE: 3D illusion

MATERIALS

screwdriver
electric sander and sanding block
primer
paintbrushes
satinwood paints
tape measure
pencil
paper or graph paper
scissors
painter's tape in two colours
artist's brush
new handles (optional)

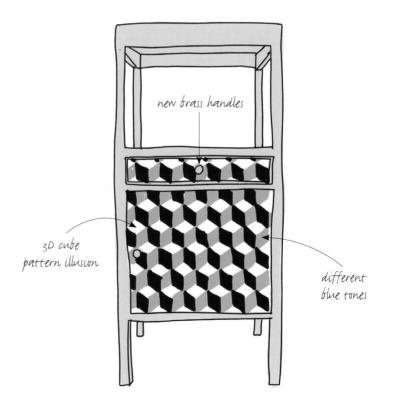

new brass handles

3D cube pattern illusion

different blue tones

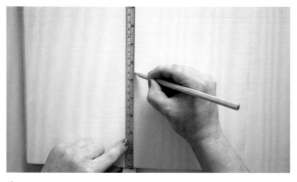

1 Take the door off its hinges and remove the hardware. The cube pattern has three colours – after preparing and priming (see page 14), apply a base coat of the lightest one, then leave to dry. Use a tape measure and pencil to mark the centre of the door, which will be the starting point for the design.

2 Draw out a perfect hexagon on a piece of paper and divide it into three equal segments, as shown here. You may find it helpful to use graph paper. Cut out the hexagon. It will be your master template for the cube pattern.

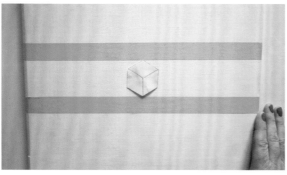

3 Work on one row of cubes at a time. Place the template on the door so that the centre of the hexagon lines up with the centre point you marked in step 2. Put down horizontal strips of yellow painter's tape above and below the template.

4 Place smaller pieces of tape around the hexagon template – I recommend using tape in a different colour, such as green, so that you don't get confused later.

5 Fold the template in half along the vertical line and put it back in place on the right-hand side, then cover the empty space on the left with yellow tape.

6 Unfold the template and fold it again, this time along the diagonal line on the right, and put it back in place so that you can finish taping off the right-hand segment, as shown here. Make sure you press the tape firmly in position.

7 Take an artist's brush and paint this segment in the lighter of your two remaining colours, which you will be using for the same segment in every cube.

8 Without waiting for the paint to dry, peel back the yellow tape to reveal your first painted segment.

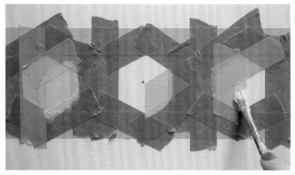

9 Repeat steps 4–8 to paint the same right-hand segment of the other cubes in this row. The space between each of these cubes should be the same width as your template so that you can fill in the gaps later. Leave to dry.

10 Repeat steps 4–8 again, but this time tape off the left-hand segment of each cube and use the darkest of your three paint colours. You may need to apply a second coat.

11 After the final coat of the darkest colour, peel back the yellow tape immediately and then leave the paint to dry.

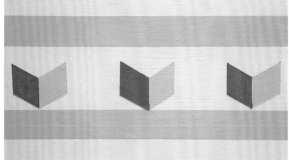

12 Peel back the green tape to reveal your first three cubes. Remember that the third segment will be left as the base colour, so you won't be able to see the full effect just yet.

13 Now it is time to add more cubes in between the ones you have already painted. Fold your template and tape around the right-hand segment with green tape, then paint with the lighter shade as in step 7. Repeat across the row.

14 Repeat the steps to paint the left-hand segment of each cube in the darkest colour as before, removing the tape after the final coat of paint. Leave to dry.

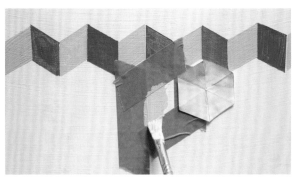

15 The rest of the pattern is going to be based on this first row. The cubes below will tessellate with the ones above, as shown here. You can now remove the two long strips of yellow tape so that you can paint the next row.

16 When painting the second row, make sure the colour above is the darker one if you're painting the lighter side and vice versa – this is how you know you are using the right colour.

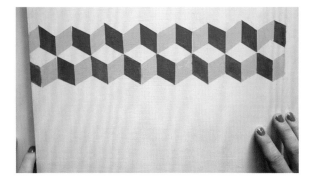

17 Continue the pattern all over the door and see the flat surface come to life in three dimensions. Leave to dry while you paint the main body of the piece in a single colour and repeat the pattern on any other doors or drawer fronts.

18 With a small artist's brush, tidy up the geometric pattern so that everything is perfectly neat. Add new handles, or simply replace the old ones.

Spell It Out

Letterboards are a great way to send messages to the people you live with. I use them at home to display positive or funny quotes. This gave me the idea of turning a chest of drawers/dresser into a giant letterboard. It would be especially lovely to make this for a child. You could share positive quotes to inspire them, wish them a happy birthday or send any other message you like as they grow up.

TECHNIQUE: letterboard

MATERIALS

screwdriver
wood filler and scraper
sanding block and electric sander
primer
paintbrushes
wooden trim (see step 2)
ruler
saw and mitre box
wood glue
hammer and tack nails
satinwood paints
Thin plywood offcuts
vinyl letter stickers (optional)

DREAM BIG

WORK HARD

LAUGH OFTEN

wooden letters
for positive quotes

letter holders are
also handles

1 Remove the old handles from the drawers. Fill the holes with wood filler, scrape off the excess and leave to dry. Sand down the filler, then prepare and prime the whole exterior (see page 14), leaving the sides of the drawers bare.

2 The trim you use to create your letterboard should look like this. It will be attached the 'wrong' way round so that it keeps the letters in place. The trim will also serve as handles for when you need to open and close the drawers.

3 Measure the width of your drawer fronts and cut several pieces of trim the same length – you will need two for each drawer. Use a mitre box for safety and accuracy. Please be sure to cut the trim carefully. Sand any rough edges.

4 Take one of the cut lengths and apply glue along the length of the trim on the side that will be facing the drawer front. Glue it in place – I used another piece of trim as a spacer at the top of the drawer to keep it level. Repeat at the bottom, then do the same with the remaining drawers.

5 Hammer in a few tack nails to hold the trim in place while the glue dries, making sure the nails are spaced evenly across the width of each drawer.

6 When the glue has dried completely, prime the trim and fill the nail holes with wood filler. Scrape off the excess and leave the filler to dry, then sand it down and prime those areas.

7 This is what the front of each drawer should look like at this stage. Measure the space between the two pieces of trim to work out how tall the letters will need to be, then paint the primed areas with two coats of satinwood paint.

MAKING THE LETTERS

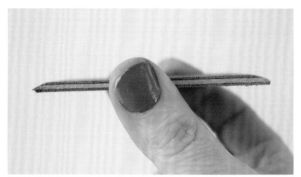

8 To make the letters, take a piece of plywood and cut it into rectangular pieces that will fit into your letterboard. You can make as many pieces as you like, depending on the size of your letterboard and how much plywood you have.

9 Sand the edges of each letter piece so that they will slide along more easily and feel smooth to the touch.

10 Paint all the letter pieces with primer and then satinwood paint. Leave to fully dry after each coat.

11 Now it's time to add the letters. I used vinyl stickers, but you could also paint them on by hand.

12 Slide in the letters one at a time to spell out words. Keep the spare letters so that you can change the message whenever you like.

Weathered and Worn

I love it when a piece of furniture tells a story. This wardrobe/armoire has a distressed, imperfect look that makes you think about its past life and where it might have been used. Applying a little Vaseline to the wood makes it easy to scrape off some of the paint later, mimicking the effects of natural wear and tear.

Wardrobes/armoires don't have to be limited to the bedroom. They can make great storage for coats and jackets in hallways. This project can get a little messy, but that's where the fun is.

TECHNIQUE: weathered paintwork

MATERIALS

screwdriver

sanding block and electric sander

wood filler (optional) and scraper

Vaseline

primer

3 jars

satinwood paints, including white

paint stir sticks

paintbrushes

stencil and stencil brushes

painter's tape

artist's brush

cleaning cloths

new handles (optional)

drill and drill bit (optional)

wallpaper and paste (optional)

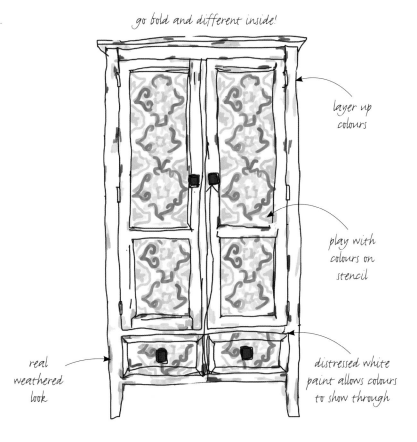

go bold and different inside!

layer up colours

play with colours on stencil

real weathered look

distressed white paint allows colours to show through

1 Remove the handles, then fill any unwanted holes left (see page 32). Prepare the whole exterior wood surface, and the interior if this will be decorated (see page 14). Put some Vaseline on the scraper and apply it to the areas where you would like the bare wood to show through.

2 Take your primer, three jars and three colours of paint. In each jar, combine three parts primer to one part paint, mixing well with a paint stir stick. Prime the wardrobe/armoire with these three different shades, allowing them to overlap. Leave to dry.

3 Use the scraper to apply a second layer of Vaseline in small areas where you would like the coloured primer to show through.

5 Secure the stencil in place with painter's tape. You can use one colour for the stencil or several – I used the same shades that I mixed with the primer in step 2. Use stencil brushes to dab the paint onto the stencil – it's important not to use normal brushstrokes, which can cause the paint to seep underneath the stencil, leading to uneven results.

4 Paint the whole piece white and leave to dry completely.

6 Work your way around the design, using a small stencil brush on the smaller details to give you greater control.

7 Peel back your stencil to reveal the pattern and move it to the next section for stencilling. Repeat until the entire piece is covered, then leave to dry. You can then use an artist's brush to tidy up the stencil design, if needed.

8 Now it is time to remove some of the paint and primer. Use the scraper to strip back all the areas where you applied Vaseline in steps 1 and 3.

9 Drag the scraper vertically across the whole piece and then horizontally, wiping the scraper on a cloth from time to time as you go. With a clean cloth, wipe away any Vaseline residue. Reattach or replace the handles (see page 32). If you like, paint and wallpaper the interior to finish (see page 62).

Resources

Joanne Condon
www.joannecondon.com
www.youtube.com/c/
  JoanneCondonDIY
Instagram: @joannecondon
I've painted thousands of pieces
of furniture over the years and
lead upcycling workshops both
face-to-face and online.

Secondhand Furniture
You can find great pieces to flip
both online and in person. See
page 9 for more tips on buying
furniture at auction or from
antique shops, thrift stores
and flea markets.

Craigslist
www.craigslist.org
*An international platform where
you can find all kinds of items for
sale in your local area.*

Ebay
www.ebay.co.uk
www.ebay.ie
www.ebay.com
*This popular auction website has
plenty of furniture bargains.*

Emmaus
www.emmaus.org.uk
*A UK charity working to end
homelessness – its shops specialize
in secondhand furniture.*

Facebook Marketplace
www.facebook.com/marketplace
*Buy and sell locally using your
Facebook account.*

Freecycle
freecycle.org
*A worldwide community where
you will find people giving away
items for free.*

Gumtree
www.gumtree.com
*Furniture, homewares and more
for sale in your area.*

Preloved
www.preloved.co.uk
*One of the UK's largest classified
advertising sites, with around
10 million members.*

Tools and Equipment
I always visit my local hardware,
interior and art stores when I am
looking for items for my projects. If
I can't find what I need there, I look
online – these are some of my
favourite brands and websites.

Amazon
www.amazon.co.uk
www.amazon.com
*For lead testing kits and any other
items you can't buy locally.*

Frog Tape
www.frogtape.com
The best quality painter's tape.

Gorilla
uk.gorillaglue.com
*All-purpose wood filler and strong
wood glue.*

Hamilton
www.hamiltondecoratingtools.co.uk
Paintbrushes and rollers.

Homestrip
www.ecosolutions.co.uk
*Solvent-free, water-based paint
strippers for home use.*

Minwax
www.minwax.com
Wood stains and finishes.

Mod Podge
www.plaidonline.com
All-in-one glue, sealer and finish.

Ronseal
www.ronseal.com
Wood fillers, stains and varnishes.

Rustins
www.rustins.ltd
*Cleaners and finishes including
sugar soap, furniture reviver and
scratch cover.*

Rust-Oleum
www.rustoleum.com
*Krud Kutter by Rust-Oleum is
one of the best cleaning products
for old furniture.*

Stencilit
www.stencilit.com
*A variety of stencils in all shapes,
sizes and styles.*

Two Fussy Blokes
www.twofussyblokes.com
High-quality microfibre rollers.

UniBond
www.unibond.co.uk
*No More Nails by UniBond is a
fast-drying wood glue.*

Paints and Primers
Water-based paints in a satinwood
or eggshell finish are the most
versatile for furniture projects –
see page 12 for more details. Try to
use a primer from the same brand
as the paint you're working with,
as they are often designed to be
used together. I explain more
about primers on page 18.

Acres Hall
www.acreshall.ie
*This Irish brand produces
high-quality handmade paints.*

Behr
www.behrpaints.com
*Behr products are sold at The
Home Depot stores across
North America.*

Colourtrend
www.colourtrend.ie
*A family-owned company with
stockists across the UK and Ireland.*

Crown
www.crownpaints.co.uk
www.crownpaints.ie
*Crown's extensive range of paints
includes satinwood, eggshell
and gloss finishes.*

Curator
www.curatorpaints.co.uk
www.curatorpaints.ie
www.curatorpaints.com
*Colours inspired by Ireland's
community of designers, makers
and artisans.*

Little Greene
www.littlegreene.com
*Heritage paints from an
independent British manufacturer.*

Sherwin-Williams
www.sherwin-williams.com
*Founded in 1866, this American
firm offers a wide variety of
paint colours.*

Handles, Hardware and Legs
A change of hardware can
completely transform a piece
– for instructions on replacing
furniture handles, see the project
Handles With Flair, from page 32.

Anthropologie
www.anthropologie.com
*Stylish drawer pulls, quirky hooks
and statement handles.*

Etsy
www.etsy.com
*Handmade and vintage designs
from sellers all over the world.*

Gipsy Hill Hardware
www.gipsyhillhardware.com
*Hand-crafted handles made from
recycled brass.*

Plank Hardware
plankhardware.com
*Affordable, design-led pieces from
a London-based company.*

Prettypegs
www.prettypegs.com
*This Swedish brand makes
alternative legs and handles for
IKEA furniture, which also work
well with non-IKEA designs.*

Wallpaper
I love using wallpaper on the
outside of a piece of furniture (see
the project On a Roll, from page
62) or as a fun surprise when you
open a drawer or cupboard.

Hygge & West
www.hyggeandwest.com
*Bold patterned papers, all made in
the US.*

Lust Home
www.lusthome.com
*Fun and joyful prints, from Art
Deco glamour to tropical motifs.*

Mini Moderns
www.minimoderns.com
*'Pattern with a story' is the motto of
this UK wallpaper brand.*

Pip Studio
www.pipstudio.com
*Classic florals and chinoiserie-
inspired designs.*

Index

Acknowledgements

To my husband Vinny, who put up a whole extra household of furniture in our home without too much complaining. You made me laugh, checked in on projects and kept me on track throughout. I'd love to say I won't be painting furniture again for a while, but I think you know me too well for that.

To my fab family, including my Mam Bernie for encouraging me since I could hold a brush. To Brian, Grace, Amy and Molly for the years of listening to ideas and getting flooded with images of painted furniture whenever I needed to ask for their opinions.

To my dear friends Catherine Keher, Santis, Karen, Catherine C, Darran and Paul, who encouraged me throughout every step and project and who I'm sure bored to tears talking about furniture but kept checking in on me.

To Mary, Louise, Marie, Lisa, Aoife, Denise, Eileen, Helen, Michelle, Holly and Mary, who probably don't even know it but kept me sane under pressure.

I would also like to thank the team at CICO Books. Thank you for your trust in my ability to bring this book to life. Huge thank you to my editor Sophie Devlin and senior commissioning editor Annabel Morgan for their patience and guidance throughout the process. To the art director Sally Powell for her sharp eye and confidence in my photography skills. To the designer Alison Fenton who made everything look so amazing. And a special thank you to the production, sales and publicity teams for their hard work behind the scenes.